# Lancashire Lasses

## THEIR LIVES AND CRIMES

*For Ted, Babs, Brad and Jayney*

## INTRODUCTION

Life for Lancashire lasses in Victorian times often followed the path from mill or mine to marriage and maternity. On average they fell pregnant eight times and would raise their children as they themselves had been raised – in grinding poverty.

The temptation to escape the hardships was too great for many. Some would turn to crime, some to the bottle and some to both. Offenders were paraded in the dock on charges ranging from picking pockets to prostitution.

Many spent their whole lives in and out of prison and in and out of the pub. Most offences were petty but, tempted by insurance money, some women committed the most heinous crime of all; deliberately murdering their husbands and children.

Lancashire Lasses is in two parts. Firstly we look at the harsh, often brutish, lives of women, their work, accommodation and limited leisure time. In the second half we follow offenders to court, prison, even to the gallows.

With many contemporary accounts and over one hundred photos/illustrations, join us in a trip back over a century to experience the lives and crimes of our Victorian ancestors.

**STEVE JONES, MARCH 2001**

First published in March 2001 by
**Wicked Publications**
222, Highbury Road, Bulwell,
Nottingham NG6 9FE, England
Telephone/Fax: (0115) 975 6828
e-mail: wickedbooks@ukonline.co.uk

© **Steve Jones 2001**

ISBN 1-870000-07-2

By the same author:

**LONDON... THE SINISTER SIDE**

**WICKED LONDON**

**THROUGH THE KEYHOLE**

**CAPITAL PUNISHMENTS**

**IN DARKEST LONDON**

**WHEN THE LIGHTS WENT DOWN**

**NOTTINGHAM... THE SINISTER SIDE**

**MANCHESTER... THE SINISTER SIDE**

**BIRMINGHAM... THE SINISTER SIDE**

**NORTHUMBERLAND AND DURHAM...
THE SINISTER SIDE**

*see back pages for details*

Typeset and printed in Great Britain by:
design②print solutions limited
9 Longwall Avenue, Nottingham NG2 1NA.

# CONTENTS

# LOW LIFE, LICENCE AND LODGING HOUSES

## IS IT THE PIG WHO MAKES THE STYE OR THE STYE WHO MAKES THE PIG?

*Men, women and children and frequently dogs form a promiscuous herd, all sleeping in the same close confined room from where every breath of pure air is excluded; while their unwashed bodies, filthy stinking clothes and frequently evil straw beds produce an atmosphere that is horrible on first entering the room. Most of the lodgers sleep in a state of absolute nudity, and decency with the greater portion of them has long ceased to be thought of.*

Manchester Inspector of Nuisances
report, 1849.

We can only guess at the goings-on beneath the lousy unwashed rags that served as bedding in Victorian Lancashire. An 1845 survey of 442 slum dwellings in Preston revealed on average almost three people to one bed. Typical would be the home of D.F., a widower, who slept in one room with his son and daughter. *The latter has a bastard child, which she affiliates on the father, he upon his son, and the neighbours on them both.*

Few details appeared in the press in cases of incest. Women and children were ordered to leave the court and the reporter told to allude to such cases as being unfit for publication. Without mentioning the charge, sketchy details did occasionally appear. In Liverpool, 1885, a mother, her son – who appeared to be about 35 – and his 16-year-old sister, were paraded before the magistrates.

The *Liverpool Review* reporter referred to the hearing as *one of those cases which cast a lurid light as of the bottomless pit on the lower classes of Liverpool*. The case collapsed through lack of evidence with no member of the family wishing to testify against another. The magistrate told the son that he left the court *with the execration of every man in it.*

The reporter was certainly pleased to see the back of him:

*Needless to say how quickly after this the horrible wretch made his way out of the dock and how careful the spectators were to avoid contact with him as he slunk rapidly towards the door.*

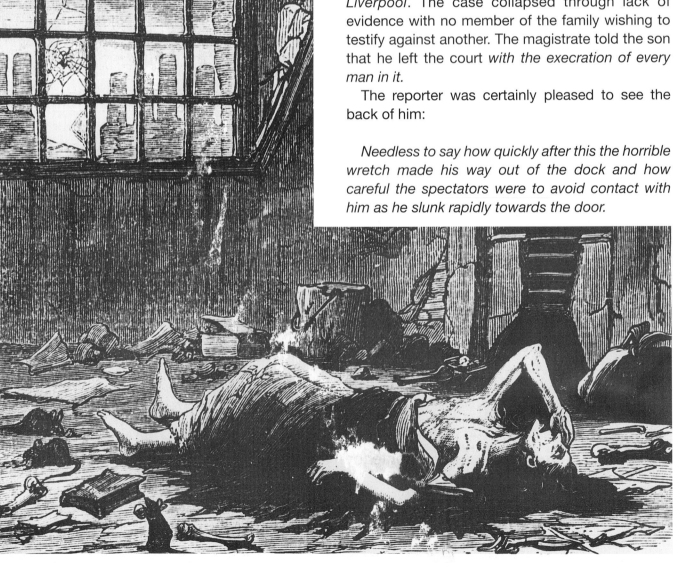

*1. The reality of Victorian values where poor pay and high rents left little money for food.*

2. Most children shared beds, sometimes with their parents. These youngsters from Accrington Street, Salford are proudly holding up the younger brothers and sisters in their care. One boy in the back row has smuggled his pet into the photo session.

Some of the saddest scenes witnessed in the police courts were played out when children were forcibly removed from the care of their parents and sent to the workhouse 'for their own safety'. Robert Blatchford witnessed such a scene in the Manchester Police Court in the 1890s. The girl's father had just been tried, probably for an offence against his own daughter. The magistrate openly rued the fact that there was little he could do in the form of direct action against the adult.

*I suppose it's no use sending you to prison. That would make no impression upon you. I'm very sorry we cannot give you a good flogging. That would do you more good than anything. I shall take the child away from you. That we can do. I wish we could order you a flogging.*

*And then he told the prisoner he could go; and the mother and child were called up again. The woman looked very anxious, the child looked very frightened. The magistrate said it was really dreadful to think of the girl being exposed to the risk* of ruin, and he should have to take her away, and send her to the workhouse where she would be properly looked after. The mother began to weep at this, said she loved her child, vowed she would take care of her; she would do better: she had worked for her all her life, she was her only comfort, and begged that the gentleman would not part them now.

*'But' said the magistrate. 'you don't take care of her. You let her sleep with you and that man who is not your husband. We cannot let this girl grow up in such a state of vice.'*

*Then the child was called into the orchestra-like well and asked her age – thirteen; and if she had slept with her father and mother for a long time? Yes.*

*The mother (weeping) said 'I have only one bed, sir; we have been sold up' but his worship was firm. 'I shall take the child away' he said.*

*Then a lady in black, a School Board lady, spoke to the child, and a constable led the mother sobbing out of the box; and – that was all.*

3. Liverpool. Women selling vegetables which were not particularly popular at the time.

Overcrowding, poverty and bed sharing, with all that implied, were the rule rather than the exception. A Salvation Army account from the 1890s lists the location of it's following report merely as 'a Lancashire town'. It was probably typical of most:

*In visiting a slum in a town our officers entered a hole, unfit to be called a human habitation – more like the den of some wild animal, almost the only furniture of which was a filthy iron bedstead, a wooden box to serve for table and chair, while an old tin did duty as a dustbin.*

*The inhabitant of this wretched den was a poor woman, who fled into the darkest corner of the place as our officer entered. The poor wretch was the victim of a brutal man who never allowed her to venture outside the door, keeping her alive by the scantiest allowance of food. Her only clothing consisted of a sack tied around her body, her hair matted and foul, presenting on the whole such an object as one could scarcely imagine living in a civilised country.*

The following description appeared in a local paper: Scotland Road, Liverpool, 1887.

*Women who were hanging about looked starved and cold, being only half-dressed. Some of them were sitting on the steps nursing children, while others were chopping chips and grinding sandstone in the dark low-roofed cellars below.*

*In a house in No.10 court, Banastre-street, which has just been papered, a young woman lived, with four young children, the eldest being six or seven years old. Her husband is dead and the only income she has is 3s a week from the parish, all of which she pays in rent. The rest she has to make up in the streets by any way that will bring in a few coppers.*

## THE DENS OF OLDHAM

Throughout the country Victorian men of the cloth set out on tours of working-class areas to expose, as they saw it, the influence of the Devil in society. It's more likely that they were frustrated voyeurs whose sole pleasures were ogling girls in a state of undress and scribbling down their 'shocking' stories. One such anonymous visitor wrote up his findings in a booklet published in 1866, *The Dens of Oldham* which set out to expose the town's *Low Lodging Houses, Thieves Dens, Common Lodging-Houses, Brothels and Prostitutes*. The main exposure, however, was of the scribe, who comes off the page as a voyeuristic vicar obsessed by vice. Let's join him in an unnamed street on the seedy side of Oldham:

*In number four were three girls, two about twenty years and the other about 14-years-old. The two eldest girls had neither shoes nor stockings on, and merely a filthy ragged petticoat full of holes and an apology for a chemise to cover their nakedness. There was not the least appearance of shame or modesty, but a reckless indifference to all feelings of shame or propriety…*

*To sit upon, there were several stones of various sizes. One was about three feet in height and might be called the sofa. The floor was a stone one, damp and filthy.*

*In the next room, on what might be called a bed, was to be seen a drunken man and a girl, whilst sitting by the fire was a woman with a small sickly emaciated child. The next room had no pretensions to furniture, unless we might call the few bricks and stones used for sitting upon by that name. There were three girls there, and a young man in all but a state of nudity. Their resting places were in the*

5. A Manchester photo with the simple title 'Woman of the Time'.

*corners of the room, nothing to protect them from the damp floor but a little straw or hay mixed with a small quantity of cotton waste.*

Our visitor's next port of call in the penurious parts of Oldham was a common lodging house where those in the tramp ward paid between 2d and 6d per night:

*In rooms where men and women sleep together the beds are divided by partitions which indeed are nothing but a mockery. They are generally made of pieces of orange or soap boxes, and the opening in some places are several inches in width. In one house a partition of that description separated the beds where lay a woman and child and a young man. Each could see what the other was doing in his or her apartment without the slightest difficulty, and there was no bar to communication between them. Brown paper and pieces of variegated wallpaper formed other divisions, but all seemed got up for the purpose of deception. How could they be otherwise, when the males and females who slept together and occupied the several beds were unmarried, and changed partners according to the whim of the moment?*

4. With so many unable to read or write gossip was a necessary means of communication.

Still not satiated our visitor finally popped into a brothel in Hanover Street, all in the name of research, of course:

*The 'girls' were preparing their supper, and there was a strong smell of bacon, mingling with that of tobacco smoke and beer. There were four in, beside two men. The men were sitting on what we called a bed post, one woman was sitting on a stone, another nursing a baby, a third cooking the supper, and a fourth lying on a piece of wood in a beastly state of intoxication, and in anything but a graceful and modest attitude. They were all more or less under the influence of drink, and the language used by them was extremely obscene and lewd, and all remains of modesty has disappeared, it was feared, for ever.*

*In another house, at a short distance off, was a masculine repulsive-looking woman, who had the reputation of being a professor in her art, and gave lessons to the youth of both sexes in debauching and wickedness.*

We'll leave the prurient priest to pay his 'prentice fees.

## ON THE ROAD

Another visitor, without a personal sex agenda, was the Secretary of the Ladies Committee at Oldham Workhouse. In the very early 1900s Mary Higgs set out to discover the accommodation available for homeless, hard up and transient women. Her undercover travels around Lancashire were revealed in *Glimpses of the Abyss* (1906).

When seeking accommodation in a workhouse tramp ward, Mary and other women were made to suffer verbal abuse known as 'bully-ragging' which was aimed by the admittance officers who would accuse them of *sponging on the rates*. Very often they would simply shoo off destitute women they considered undesirable. One regular applicant was told: *Get out with you, you ____ !* and *Off with you ____ sharp.*

On the night Mary and her friend arrived they were told they would have to stay two nights and pick three pounds of oakum. After bathing in six inches of water, both women were frisked for pipes and tobacco before being admitted to their sleeping quarters:

*We were then marched into the large dormitory and told to let down a wide board propped against the wall, one for each. A row of sleeping women occupied similar 'plank beds'. There were a few straw beds on bedsteads, but only for sick folks, and also some children's cribs.*

With one blanket below and two above, neither of the two visitors could generate enough warmth to sleep. There were also other more unsavoury reasons for their insomnia:

*Your neighbour breathed right in your face, and you had all the twisting and turning of a sufferer on each side to add to your own. Most of the women had colds, and you succumbed yourself under the double influence of contagion and chillness. Then your coughing and sneezing added to the common misery…*

*One newcomer was a poor old granny, very bad with rheumatism, accused of drink. This old woman sighed, groaned and moaned 'Oh deary me! Lord help us' most of the night and was in real pain. She got out of bed twice with numerous sighs and groans, taking a quarter of an hour at least each time.*

*Bed after bed was let down and dragged across the floor… someone was constantly wandering to the adjoining lavatory or sitting up or coughing or moving uneasily.*

The accommodation had to be paid for by work. After rising at 5.30am and breakfasting on gruel, Mary was given her tasks:

*I was taken away after two hours' oakum picking and set to clean. I was provided with materials, shown where to get water and set to clean. 'scrub, mind you' the lavatories, the W.C.s and a staircase with three landings and three flights of stairs. I was also to clean the paint in the lavatories.*

Lunch consisted of a little bread and cheese and tea, and the evening meal – gruel and dry bread – was followed by an early night in the dormitory.

On her travels Mary had nothing but praise for the Salvation Army hostels but found the lodging houses, at 6d a night, a little on the expensive side. With her friend she budgeted for the day's spending:

*We laid out our scanty resources as follows: tea 1d, sugar 1d, bread 3d, butter 2d. Not being hungry we decided to go to the common sitting room. This we found in possession of several women, mostly young. It was now nearing 10pm and they were all busy*

6. *Gerard Street, Liverpool where whole families would sleep in one room and shoes were a luxury.*

*tidying themselves, rouging their faces, blacking their eyelids and preparing to go on the streets. All this was done perfectly openly and their hair was curled by the fireside. It was wonderful how speedily they emerged from slatterns into good-looking young women. Each then sallied forth...*

*The inmates, probably about sixty, young and old, were living a life of sin, and we were told that the proprietor of this lodging-house owned fifteen others. Most of the girls came home very late – many as late as two o' clock – and in such a state that they kept the others awake, singing and talking, drunk or maudlin. The house was open till two at any rate every night.*

*At breakfast round the fire was a group of girls far gone in dissipation; good-looking girls most of them, but shameless; smoking cigarettes, boasting of drinks, or drinking, using foul language, singing music-hall songs or talking vileness. The room grew full, and breakfasts were about; onions, bacon, beefsteak, tea etc filling the air with mingled odours. A girl called Dot and another danced 'the cake-walk' in the middle of the floor.*

*7. China Lane, Lancaster, looking south (1890s). The lane contained many densely populated lodging houses.*

Many of the lodgers had abandoned themselves to drink. A 'scotch' woman, genteel in appearance, boasted to the two visitors that she had been drunk every day for more than a week. Inebriates caused the majority of problems. One of the most notorious was 'Mussel Woman' who wandered the streets carrying an empty basket on her arm. She was no Molly Malone, however, the basket had never seen a shellfish, her livelihood was all a fantasy. Having no money to pay for accommodation was no impediment to mussel woman, as she would regularly present herself at the lodging-house and demand admission. When refused entry she threatened to stand outside and *keep shouting all night*. She was as good as her word. For the next half hour she screamed *the most abusive personal language* whilst pounding all the while on the door. The determined Scot would only desist for a few minutes when a policeman passed by, and, after two hours, she was begrudgingly allowed entry.

Unmarried women with low incomes and without mussel woman's persuasive powers were forced to share rooms in the marginally cheaper unlicensed 'lodging houses'. Details of one such establishment came to light when an Inspector of Nuisances made a midnight spot inspection to assess the sleeping arrangements. In 1874, Jane Shaw's home at 9, Matthias's buildings was assessed by Robert Williamson. It consisted of just two rooms. Upstairs the inspector found seven women sheltering together with barely space to breathe in one tiny room. Five said they were full-time lodgers and paid two shillings each weekly. The other two were casuals. The house was not registered and nor would it be, being deemed unfit. Jane pleaded poverty and implored the bench to be lenient. She was fined an immediate two shillings and sixpence and five shillings for every day the house remained unregistered. Shaw was done for.

Poverty was the principle cause of ill-health and consumption and abscesses were common problems, usually treated at home. District nurses were therefore privy to some of the most heartrending cases of atrocious housing. In Liverpool 1866, a nurse was called to a mother of two, who had been deserted by her husband and was living in a room 9ft square. All the furniture had been pawned or sold for food and the bed was a sack of straw on which the three huddled for warmth. The older daughter was sent to beg on the streets and, in the absence of the district nurse, the mother relied on her younger, six-year-old daughter to dress her abscesses.

The standard of medical care depended very much upon the pounds and pennies in the purse.

# FROM THE CRADLE TO THE (EARLY) GRAVE

8. Selling cast off clothing in Fox Street, Liverpool. Let's hope the young mother on the right was able to find an affordable pair of shoes. (Is this the same young lady the centre of attention on photo No. 6?).

With little or no sexual education, couples were left in the dark and did what came naturally. A young woman in Barrow, forced into marriage because of her pregnancy, was told by a relation: *You have been tasting soup before it was ready,* to which she replied, *yes, and I found a carrot in it.*

A Bolton woman, born in 1903, remembers the ignorance and shame concerned with anything 'down there':

*She [mother] didn't tell us anything about that [sex] you didn't know where babies came from… you didn't have sanitary things then, you just had to wear old clothes or anything and put them in a bucket. They used to say 'Don't let your brother see that.'*

9. *The Victorian equivalent of a boot sale in Fox Street, Liverpool. Market stalls cost money so vendors simply spread out their wares, themselves and their children on the pavement.*

The most common forms of birth control in Victorian Lancashire were probably abstinence – which certainly didn't make the heart grow fonder – and withdrawal – not going all the way to Blackpool but getting off the bus at South Shore. Many children were not planned or wanted but nonetheless arrived in their numbers as, even within marriage, most couples did not fully understand when babies might be conceived. Girls taking a gamble outside wedlock risked losing a lot more than their virginity.

In villages, where everyone knew everyone else's business, falling pregnant when still single was viewed as the ultimate sin. Former friends and relations would avert their eyes and cross the road at the sight of an unmarried expectant mother.

Some pregnant single girls in Victorian Liverpool were packed off to mental hospitals, where, completely friendless, they were treated as if they had committed the most heinous of crimes. A sign on the institution wall stated "Lunatics and Idiots allowed visitors". Young expectant mothers didn't fit this category and therefore never viewed a friendly face nor heard the tender words of encouragement we all need in hard times. Instead, in some institutions, they were banished to the penitentiary and forced to spend hours on their knees begging forgiveness.

Women in all walks of life sought abortions. In 1859 Dr. Charles Clay, Senior Medical Officer at St Mary's Hospital, Manchester, did a survey of the 790 women in his hospital and private practice, who had passed child-bearing age. He found that 430, more than half, had both given birth and had abortions; 350 mothers had never had abortions. Only 10 women in the practice had had neither children nor abortions.

The total number of pregnancies for the group of 790 was 6,970, which meant a woman, on average, fell pregnant about eight times. For every seven children born, one was aborted. Indeed one woman confessed to having had 23 terminations.

In interviews with working Victorian mothers a surprisingly high number found pregnancy less arduous than might be expected for the times. Nearly all interviewees bemoaned their families' low wages, which both kept them short of food and forced them to work almost up to giving birth.

For those not in employment the family bed was brought downstairs a fortnight before the baby was due. From this vantage point, expectant mothers ruled the roost, doing what jobs they could, like pealing potatoes and knitting and delegating the other chores to reluctant children and other helpers.

The most common complaints were related to swollen legs and feet, varicose veins and doctors, who when they could be afforded, often arrived drunk or diseased. Midwives carried less infection with them, but doctors had instruments, which, in an emergency, could save lives. You literally paid your money and took your choice. Midwives were paid about £2, but for some even this fee was too expensive and babies were born with the assistance of 'wise women'. Although the location is not given, the following account of a Victorian mother's life, composed in reply to a questionnaire, would be fairly typical for Lancashire:

10. Everybody enjoyed a good cuppa. Fox Street again, the forerunner to Paddy's Market, Scotland Road.

11. Selling crockery c1890. This was probably a cracking trade to be in judging by the number of domestic disputes reported in court during which both cups and saucers were flying.

12. *Haggling and penny-pinching were economic necessities of life in Liverpool.*

13. *Fish Market, Great Charlotte Street, Liverpool c1895.*

## THE TERRIBLE SUFFERING I ENDURED

*The first part of my life I spent in a screw factory from six in the morning till five at night; and after tea used to do my washing and cleaning. I only left two weeks and three weeks before my children were born.*

*After that I took in lodgers and washing, and always worked up till an hour or so before the baby was born. The results are that three of my girls suffer with their insides. None are able to have a baby. One dear boy was born ruptured on account of my previous hard work... I can only look back now on the terrible suffering I endured, that tells a tale now upon my health. I could never afford a nurse, and so was a day or two after my confinements obliged to sit up and wash and dress the others.*

*My husband's wages varied owing to either hot weather or some of the other men not working. I have known him come home with £3 or £4 and I have seen him come home with nothing; and when earning good money, as much as 30s, has been paid away in drink.*

*I had three little ones in two years and five months, and he was out of work two years, and during that time I took in washing and sewing and have not been near a bed for night after night. I was either at my sewing-machine or ironing after the little ones had gone to bed. After being confined five days I have had to do all for my little ones. I worked sometimes up till a few moments before they were born.*

*WAGES £3 or £4 to nothing; ten children, two miscarriages.*

Until the end of the 1800s, following delivery, midwives and grandmothers kept up the traditional practice of forcing the new mother, wrapped in blankets, to perspire in front of a blazing fire. Regularly plied with voluminous cups of ale or stout, she was fed on gruel for four days after the birth. Mothers sometimes stopped in bed for up to ten days after birth with a binder to flatten the stomach. Part of the midwife's duty was to tighten this binder as well as bath the baby.

The risk of infection often made hospital births more dangerous than home ones. Poor hospital design sometimes led to patients feeling worse than they had at home. In the 1850s a ventilation shaft at Manchester Royal Infirmary conducted smells from the mortuary throughout the female surgical wards. The WCs were ventilated directly into the wards pervading them with a penetrating and sickly odour.

By the standards of the 1860s, women giving birth in Liverpool Workhouse Hospital, two thirds of whom were unmarried, were particularly well cared for. The maternal death rate of 1 in 250 was comparatively very low. In fact, Liverpool, because of its generous provision of fully trained midwives and trainee obstetric nurses, was one of the safest places in the country to give birth. Unfortunately for those with difficult labours, there was early resistance to some new ideas, it being observed that *women used obscene language under chloroform.*

Liverpool's lying-in hospital had to be abandoned in 1882 because of endemic erysipelas and puerperal fever. Scarlet fever and smallpox were also rampant. It was eventually discovered that the hospital's drains ran uphill.

14. The Rag Market. Wages were so low that Liverpool became a city of 'second-hand Roses'.

Almost one in four mothers was in full-time employment in the late nineteenth century thus occasioning a demand for child minders. Grandmothers were the first natural choice, followed by other relations, friendly neighbours, lodgers and professional child minders. Most babies, given the harsh times, were looked after as well as could be expected though the odd horrendous story came out. On occasions, for example, minders were discovered tying children to chairs all day – however tempting, don't try this at home!

15. *The first baby show was held in Manchester with the 4-month-old winner weighing in at just under two stone. This photo Salford Maternity Training School.*

## BREAST IS BEST

With mill work being relatively well paid, pregnant workers stayed in their jobs almost to the onset of contractions and were eager to return as soon as possible after giving birth. Often babies were brought to the factories and mills for feeding. Walter Greenwood recalls such a scene from pre-WW1 Salford:

*The babies in the pram were screeching though their howlings were inaudible. I saw Mr Wheelam take out his watch and stand with it in his hand as he looked upwards through the window at the mill buzzer conspicuous above the engine house. A white jet of vapour steam under pressure plumed forth and another shrill note was added to the general discord. Weavers threw the driving belts on to the idler pulleys; the deafening clatter stopped abruptly though its echoes still pounded my ears. A burst of chatter, a clattering of clogs as the weavers lined up with pint mugs at a gas geyser and brewed tea. The mothers claimed their screaming offspring, sat on the floor by the looms and began to suckle their infants while friends put steaming pints of tea at their sides and whatever it was had been brought to eat.*

To encourage breast feeding the first baby show in Britain was held in Manchester in 1905 with the object of finding 'the heaviest and fattest babies'.

The four-month-old winner, dressed solely in a 'clout' (nappy), weighed in at twice the then norm – an astonishing 23lbs!

A Preston man, born in 1884, remembers seeing a woman employing a 'breast exhauster' to draw off her milk:

*I actually remember seeing one and it was like a rubber teat and that was squeezed and it would draw so much milk out of the breast and it would fall into a container underneath. But what happened to it afterwards, whether it got to the baby or not I don't know. I had a friend a bit older than me who told me of his mother having a baby in the mill and feeding it in the mill while she was working.*

## MASSACRE OF THE INNOCENTS

Concealing the birth of a child, even if born prematurely and dying of natural causes, was an offence. No social level of society was unaffected by the problem of unwanted children and, to their eternal shame, members of the middle class were occasionally paraded in the dock.

In Liverpool, 1880, a 38-year-old married bookseller, Edwin Ovenden stood before the court. His co-accused were Marianne Gray, a young widow *of pleasing appearance* and Mary Anne Bretton, her mother, both from West Derby. The two

16

ladies were charged with the concealment of a child born to Marianne. Her lover, Edwin, whose wife kept a stationers in Berry Road, was charged with assisting in the concealment of a baby boy. The three accused must have wondered how they ever came to be in this position as they were the only people ever to know of the existence of the premature boy. They must have cursed their luck as the trial progressed.

A few months earlier the body of an abandoned baby girl had been found in an entry off Norwood Grove. This would not have created one small fraction of the public interest it would today, but the policeman whose case it became, was a dogged sort of fellow. Acting on a hunch, he scoured the local paper for an advertisement for a wet nurse which led him to Marianne Gray. Following some hostile questioning as to how she could advertise her services as a wet nurse yet produce no baby of her own, Marianne and her mother were charged with the concealment of the baby girl, the discovery of whose body he was investigating. The only way the barmaid could prove her innocence of the charge was by telling the truth. Marianne confided to the startled policeman that she had in fact given birth, after a five month confinement, not to the baby girl, but to a baby boy that lived for just a few minutes. The body was passed on to its father for disposal.

The jury listened attentively as the prosecution outlined how Edward Ovenden secreted the remains in a cigar-box 9"x5"x5" and took it in an omnibus to the Mersey. Reaching the pierhead he accidentally left the box (which also had a stone in it) on the bus. He ran back and retrieved his grisly load, and, boarding one of the Woodside boats, then dropped the box into the water. The existence of the young child had previously only ever been known to the three accused.

Upon hearing this evidence Marianne's father fainted in court. A few seconds later she too collapsed under the strain. Despite restoratives being administered, she remained in a semi-conscious state for the rest of the trial. Having recovered during the 40 minutes that the jury took to deliberate, it would have come as no surprise if Marianne had collapsed a second time when the judge passed sentence. Both Marianne and Ovenden, the child's father, were sentenced to a relatively harsh four months. Her mother was acquitted.

In the same court 16-year-old domestic servant Mary Rutter waited apprehensively for her sentence to be handed down. She too was charged with endeavouring to conceal the birth of a child. In a panic, Mary had wrapped the body of her stillborn baby in paper and placed it in an unlocked box in her place of employment in Walton Road. Discovered by her employers, the police were called in. The father was her previous employer. Found guilty, there was a strong recommendation to mercy and Mary was sentenced to just four days – which she had already served on remand. Mary left the court a free woman. Her present employer was as good as the previous was bad: Mary was promptly re-engaged.

Mary Rutter was probably leniently treated because of her youth. Another Mary, Mary McCahill, also in service, was less fortunate. Having secreted her baby under a grate in the cellar of her home in Broughton Lane, Manchester she was sentenced to three months with hard labour. Mary McCahill was 27 and the court clearly considered she should have known better.

## WHILE THE BALANCE OF HER MIND WAS DISTURBED

40-year-old weaver John Rushton and his 38-year-old wife Harriett were the traditional poor but honest folk who populated 1880s Colne. Not for them whole evenings squandered in alehouses with their children languishing in squalor at home. Both were chapel goers. John was generally acknowledged as 'a decent man' and Harriett 'one of the cleanest and tidiest of women'. The seven year marriage was considered one of the happiest in town.

One Saturday afternoon, the weather being fine, the couple and their two daughters and son, upon whom they doted, spent the day rambling in Tum Hills. Back home in their cottage, with a healthy appetite induced by the fresh air and exercise, the family sat down to their evening meal in the usual way. At about 6pm John kissed his daughters (4 and 3) and son (1) goodbye as he set off for the sick club at the chapel. Harriett reminded him to buy the normal provisions.

In the trim and prim cottage at Lenches, Harriett Rushton carried her children one by one into the back room and quickly, silently and methodically dispatched them into eternity. Not a sound was heard by the neighbours. The rent collector called as two children lay lifeless in the back room. Noticing that Mrs Rushton was 'excited' he pocketed his money and informed her that the rent was to be raised by 2d the following week. She paid him in silence and made no comment about the increase. After he left the mother completed her grisly job and then carefully arranged her three children, Mary Jane, Martha Ann and William Wendle on the bed. The lifeless bodies were laid side by side and neatly covered with bedclothes. Mrs Rushton changed her dress and shoes, locked the house and made the short journey to her sister's.

Here she placed the key in the dresser and told her sister to pass it on to her husband. When asked where the children were Harriett calmly replied:

*They are in heaven. I know your child was in heaven and I wanted mine to go there too.*

Harriet's nephew had died of natural causes five weeks previously and she had been extremely depressed ever since. John Rushton, her husband, was sent for. Together with the police and a doctor, visibly shaking, he entered the cottage where his worst fears were confirmed; there, fully clothed except for their clogs, lay his lifeless children whose once warm lips had kissed him goodbye just a few hours previously.

All three tiny necks displayed rope marks and the clothes line used to strangle them lay discarded across the room.

There appeared no motive for the crime. Harriett's mother had hanged herself two years previously and her brother drowned himself in Faulconbridge reservoir. Another brother was in an asylum where poor Harriett was destined to join him. Found guilty of murder at the coroner's court, Mrs Rushton was found unfit to plead at the Assizes and ordered to be detained at Her Majesty's pleasure.

## WETTING THE BABY'S HEAD

The Victorians definitely had something about babies and boxes. Just two days after giving birth in Preston in 1858, Jane Parker was proudly presenting her new born son to the locals in the Black-a-Moors Head pub in Lancaster Road. She was wetting the baby's head with a gin and water. From the hostelry Jane went to a furniture brokers in Friargate and ordered a small travelling box and a direction tag.

Popping her son into the box, she sealed it and attached the tag with an address in Liverpool. In another pub she gave the parcel, along with 3d for his troubles, to a labourer to take to the railway station. The box was delivered the next day to the surprise and horror of the addressee, a Mrs Melville, whose connection with the defendant has never been revealed. She later told the court that she believed the little boy was still just holding on to life and tried to revive him by warming him in front of the fire. The child was pronounced dead upon arrival at the Northern Dispensary.

Diligent police work led police officers to Jane Parker's home. Spotting the uniformed officers she rushed into the kitchen and put a small bottle to her lips and attempted to gulp down its contents. Having swallowed little more than a spoonful, the liquid was quickly snatched and the laudanum put out of harm's way.

In her defence Jane argued that she had been told by the ubiquitous 'man in the pub' that a child could live for two days in a box. She admitted to having given her two-day-old son some gin to help him sleep on the journey. With the charge being reduced from murder to manslaughter, Jane Parker pleaded guilty and was sentenced to six months with hard labour.

## THE LOWEST OF THE LOW

It can be argued that even more horrific crimes were committed by adults of supposedly sound mind against children. In Liverpool, as elsewhere, there was a widespread belief that VD could be cured by having intercourse with a virgin child. There were practically no depths to which female procuresses would not sink to meet the demands of this foul trade. Some set themselves up as quacks and kept special brothels in Liverpool to provide the 'cure' for VD sufferers. Many of the very young girls forced to perform this service were imbeciles who quickly became infected themselves. Three admitted to Liverpool Lock Hospital were aged just 9, 7 and 5-years-old. Thus, born mentally sub-normal, they were raped and infected with venereal disease before their tenth birthday.

Those not willing to pay at the child brothels simply abducted girls on the streets. A man with *very bad syphilitic ulcers* raped a 14-year-old girl. He defended himself in court by saying he had meant her no harm. The only reason for his actions was to rid himself of disease.

Amos Green committed a similar offence on a girl of nine. Her parents were illiterate, and, when they noticed sores on the girls genitals, they believed these to have been caused by their daughter swallowing a sixpenny piece. They were reluctant to give evidence against Green.

16. In 1858, Jane Parker wet her baby's head with a gin and water in the Black-a-Moors Head in Preston. Later she wrapped up the child in a parcel and posted it off to Liverpool. The baby was just clinging on to life when it arrived but pronounced dead after being rushed to the Northern Dispensary.

## AN EARLY EXIT

Premature deaths were not the sole preserve of children. Many women popped their clogs at a relatively early age due to alcoholism. For many the first and last mention in newspapers was a report of their premature death. Evidence of way of life is often unearthed when investigating the cause of death. Typical notes from cases coming before the coroner's court in Liverpool, 1880, included the following:

*Mary Edwards, 47, No.8 Circus Street. Deceased was addicted to drink. Visited house of cousin at 5, Hunter street. Under influence at midnight. Seen to be leaving house to go home. Found on face on parlour floor. Quite dead. Jury found deceased died from suffocation.*

*Maria Quinlan, 23, found dead in a house in Pellew street. Deceased was an unfortunate who had been drinking every day with a Spanish seaman*

*named Peter Byzanti with whom she cohabited. Another unfortunate said she heard the Spaniard say that he would put deceased in her coffin. The medical men found she died 'with a drinker's liver'. Verdict accordingly.*

*Mary Vince, 56, wife of P.C. at 16, St Hilda street. Friday 9.30pm deceased's husband went to bed leaving wife knitting in kitchen. He fell asleep, woke at 2am and found wife at bottom of stairs – accidental death.*

*Hannah E Angel, 43, from 39, Dryburgh street. For a long period had given way to excessive drinking of spirits, taking spells lasting as long as three or four months. Had been drinking consistently for previous six weeks and neglected to take food. Found dead in bed on Saturday afternoon with clothes on. Husband stated she had not been undressed for a fortnight. Repeatedly got drunk, slept the effects of drink off and then got drunk again. Died from effects of excessive drinking.*

*Annie Harrison, 25, 17, Alexandra street. Was in the habit of taking chlorodine under medical treatment. On Friday husband returned home and found her insensible. Bottle which had contained chlorodine found empty. Doctor called in – too late. Death caused by overdose of chlorodine.*

*Mary Molloy, 17, 2, Woodstock street. Left home, slept rough for three weeks. Seen with several other girls sitting around some hot cinders at the alkali works in Lightbody street. Later seen kneeling on cinders with her head resting on her arms, apparently asleep. Great quantity of smoke blown into her face. Other girls did not help saying she was suffering from toothache. Found dead through suffocation caused by inhaling carbonic acid gas from the cinders in question.*

In Dundas Street, Bootle, Mary McKay was chopping wood in the yard when a portion of iron guttering from the roof fell upon her head crushing her skull.

Mary Clare of Wilfer Street, Edgehill took another way out. Her husband returned about midnight, gaining access through a window to find his wife hanging from the bannisters; she had been dead some 16-17 hours. Evidence was given that her husband was drunk on the night in question. Verdict: *Died from suffocation.* There was insufficient evidence to show Mary's state of mind.

Henrietta Whale, 41, the wife of a 'licensed victualler' in Stanley Road, Liverpool was found by her husband hanging from a rope tied to a clothes hook in the wardrobe. As the report says 'she was quite dead'. Eighteen months previously she had been bitten by a dog and had convinced herself she was dying of hydrophobia. Verdict: *suicide while in a state of temporary mental derangement.*

**SHOCKING SUICIDE.**

*17. 1874 saw a suicide mania in Salford. Attempting to fly from an upstairs window was less popular than a long dip in the canal.*

## AN END TO IT ALL

In the 1870s sentences for attempted suicide were between six and twelve months, more of an incentive to do the job properly than a deterrent. Residents of Salford seemed to be amongst the most likely to top themselves. 1874 was a particularly bad year with headlines in the newspaper running *The Suicide Mania in Salford.* Self-destruction seemed almost fashionable as in one week alone Anne Chapel, a 55-year-old servant tried to hang herself and Edith Hope (seamstress), Alice Nugent (charwoman), Rose Elliott (boatwoman) and Mary Davies (servant) were all rewarded with 6-12 months inside for similarly failed attempts.

One year later, Caroline Wilkinson tried to end it all by hanging herself in the police office of Salford Town Hall. She had staggered in some minutes previously and told the officer that she imagined somebody running after her. Caroline was allowed to sit on a form in the reserve room. When the officer next saw her she was hanging from a scarf which had been fastened to a hook. Cut down and charged, Caroline revealed that attempting suicide in police stations was something of a hobby of hers. Revealing a long scar on her neck she stunned the officials by casually stating: *It's not so bad as when I cut my throat in Manchester.* At her trial Caroline told the court that she could recall none of the events as she had been drinking all day.

A favoured method of self-destruction was to throw oneself into the River Irwell. Sentencing was not consistent. Three women pulled out in 1875 were typical cases. Thirty-year-old Elizabeth Dodd took the plunge because her brother had been beating her for not providing him with any eggs. She

AWFUL SUICIDE AT BOLTON

*18. Mary Hogg was sent home from service through illness in 1884. She went to the hot water reservoir and, shouting to a stranger 'You'll know where to find me if you want me' threw herself into the water. Her body was recovered after the reservoir was dragged.*

was bound over in the sum of £20 to keep the peace and her brutish brother sent down for six months. Elizabeth Kinsella, a domestic servant, could see no future for herself when her mistress refused her a reference while Ann Fielding, a 60-year-old charwoman, was simply tired of life; both women had twelve months in which to reflect upon their failure to feed the fish.

## A DIP IN THE LEEDS AND LIVERPOOL

In the latter years of the century, although still against the law, those who 'failed' were rarely punished. Ada Pritchard, a 16-year-old from Rishton, was just one of many who saw her name in print in 1892.

One Saturday morning at Victoria Mill, Ada, between sobs, blurted out to her best friend, Sarah Clegg, that she was going to throw herself in the Leeds and Liverpool canal. She had only earned 4s 9d that week and was terrified that her father would thrash her.

Sarah recruited five friends who, after work, followed the depressed Ada along the canal bank towards Tottleworth Bridge. As she prepared to jump in the girls rushed her and managed to prevent her from taking her life. As she was led back to the mill, Ada simply said she would do it another time. A

P.C. Knight was called in, and, when told about the father's beating of his daughter, paid him a visit. Mr Pritchard said that he had not thrashed his daughter for at least two years but had had words with her that morning. The case eventually ended up in court where the father told magistrates exactly what he had said when his daughter could not find a brush he had asked her for:

*You great gormless b_____ you can see nothing d_____you, get off to the factory or you will be late.*

From the bench Mr Openshaw opined that this was not quite the proper language he should use to his daughter.

Perhaps the suicide attempt was a cry for help as Ada later revealed that she had been the frequent receiver of thrashings from her father's belt as he suspected her of bringing lads home. Surprisingly Ada was remanded in custody for a week, possibly to protect her from herself. The police were ordered to look into the allegations against her father.

Life was not all doom and gloom and most girls of Ada's age found ways of amusing themselves.

# WORK, REST AND PLAY

19. *A very rare photo of a pub interior. Young girls and boys were often forced by their parents to entertain the locals for a few pence.*

Women of every generation remember with affection the games they played and songs they sang in school playgrounds or on the streets. Some of the rhymes and ditties were about famous murder cases; others tell us more about the living conditions. Most importantly, whether they made sense or not, they were fun.

One particularly popular game was played with a mother (a girl acting the role) and her daughters and friends. The girls would dance forward twice chanting *Buy me a pair of milking cans, milking cans, milking cans, Oh mother o' mine.*

The 'mother' would reply *Where shall we get the money from, money from, money from? (repeat) Oh daughter o' mine.* The 'daughters' would then respond *Sell my father's bedsocks, bedsocks bedsocks* etc. The game might continue along the following pattern:

'Where will your father sleep?' 'Sleep in mother's bed'
'Where will your mother sleep? 'Sleep in the girl's bed'
'Where will the girls sleep? 'Sleep in the boys' bed'
'Where will the boys sleep? 'Sleep in the pig-cote'
'Where will the pigs sleep?' 'Sleep in the dolly tub'
'Where shall I wash in?' 'Wash in the thimble'
'What shall I sew with?' 'Sew with the poker'
'What shall I poke the fire with?' 'Poke it with your finger'
'What shall you say if I burn myself?' 'Serve you right, serve you right'

This final line was the signal to scatter as the cheeky daughters were chased by a churlish mother.

The following song became very popular with Lancashire lassies but was frowned upon by their teachers:

*There was a lady, a lady o*
*And she was courting a joiner o*
*She did her best to let no one know*
*That she was courting a joiner o*
*And when her father got to know*
*Her rosy cheeks they turned as white as snow,*
*He took a stick and beat her so*
*And then he ordered her to bed to go.*
*She went upstairs so full of woe*
*She hung herself from the cupboard o*
*And when next morning they cut her down,*
*Hidden in her bosom this note was found*
*Oh William, William dear, I love thee well,*
*I love thee better than tongue can tell.*

Children would wander the streets singing odd little jingles to themselves:

*Oliver Cromwell lost his shoe*
*In the battle of Waterloo*
*Sent his wife to Botany Bay*
*Where she sang Ta-ra-boom-de-ay*

*Eenie meenie minie mo,*
*Put the baby on the poe*
*When it's done, wipe its bum*
*Eenie, meenie, minie mo.*

*My father is a school-board man,*
*He catches all the kids he can,*
*He grabs 'em by the collar*
*An' he makes 'em pay a dollar.*
*My father is a school-board man.*

*Pancake Tuesday's a very happy day,*
*If you don't give us a holiday, we'll all run away.*
*Where will you run to? Down Moss Lane*
*I'll tell teacher and you'll get the cane.*

THE·BELGIAN·SPIN·MILL·CARDROOM·HANDS·TAKEN·MARCH·1904

*20. Girls were going out to work when barely in their teens. Despite the long hours they still had enough energy for a little fun and frolicking before marriage and maternity.*

For many families school attendance was low on their list of priorities. In the perennial effort to make ends meet, children would be withdrawn to help with the harvest or look after younger siblings. An example of the total disregard for education is displayed in the head teacher's log book from St Paul's school, Halliwell in 1897:

*Mrs Turlington came into the school this morning at 11.45 and called to her Robert in a loud voice to at once leave his class and take his uncle's dinner to him. I pointed out that this is contrary to the regulations, but the woman told the boy to disregard me and at once leave the school, which he did.*

21. *Possibly the happiest years of their lives. Young girls entertained themselves with street games, songs and skipping. Richmond Road, Liverpool c1895.*

## 'DIRTY MARY' AND FRIENDS

For teenage workers fairs were often the highlight of the year. Despite the author's obvious reservations, the booklet, *Liverpool Life*, published in 1849, captures the sheer joy of living and being young. It's available in Liverpool Central Reference Library and well worth a read. Let's join the youngsters at the fair on the swinging boat:

*Many young lasses, seeing the boat in motion, ran into the yard. Although joyous in their manner, they all use fearful language in addressing each other. Girls of tender years are swearing in their play; the proprietor of the boat is swearing professionally. Boys are pulling on the ropes, which send the boat on gaily. The ladies in the boat, not yet satisfied with the speed, cry out for increased exertion. One modest creature prefaces her request by _____ the eyes and limbs of 'Billy', a friend for whom she appears to have a special regard, as she threatens to decapitate him immediately on her descent from the car. The next moment she changes her mind, and instead of urging an increase in speed she requests 'Billy' to drop it. Billy is only one of the group of rope-pullers, and, however well disposed he may be to 'drop it' he cannot control his fellow-labourers, who pull away vigorously.*

*The young lady then, with a loud and lusty voice, which she makes heard far above the din around, screams out 'Hold on, you _____ fool; don't you see 'Dirty Mary' coming?'*

*The boat is immediately stopped, and two dirty young women in tatters enter the yard. One of them is 'Dirty Mary;' and it is only doing her fair justice to observe that in personal appearance, language, and so far as we have the opportunity of judging, in disposition, she fully justifies the cognomen. A new crew now gets on board the boat. Dirty Mary with her dirty companion, with several other dirty and ragged girls and two young men, are seated, and away goes 'The Bloomer.' amidst the laughter of the crowd and the joy of its cargo. When the vessel is fairly under way the young men begin to 'tittle' the girls whose drapery is thereby disturbed. Nevertheless their laughter becomes furious.*

*On this subsiding, yells and fearful curses are heard. 'By _____ , I'll pitch you out.' 'Go to _____, you dirty-faced cur' and many other less innocent and playful compliments are passed. A coarse song is now commenced by one of the ladies, the disgusting burden of chorus of which is taken up by all hands, and in such trim does the Bloomer sail away with its living freight of guilt and immorality.*

Other than time spent at fairs, free leisure for a little fun and frolicking was at a premium. For most folk pleasure was confined to evenings and rest days during the years prior to marriage and maternity. In 1899 a factory girl told the *Social Gazette* that she earned eight shillings a week and of this gave seven to her mother. On Sundays she

22. One of the greatest pleasures was dressing up to go out on a Saturday night. Glad rags would be taken out of the pawnshop and returned the following Monday morning.

23 Reality and fantasy. This kind of postcard was extremely popular in the early years of the twentieth century.

24. Workers at a quilt manufacturers in Eccles c1910. An interesting photo for followers of fashion as the workers have donned their best clothes for the cameraman. It's hard to believe that the girls in the front row have by now finished their schooling.

would get up at 1pm and spend 'a jolly hour or two' in a pub with the lads. The newspaper – published by the Salvation Army – appeared to disapprove of how most lasses spent their leisure time. Described as being *carelessly dressed, wearing heavy earrings and hats decked with outrageous finery and feathers* factory girls in the larger towns and cities would go out on the razzle:

*After the day's work she seeks enjoyment wherever it may be found. The enjoyment may be of a low order, such as dancing on the streets to the tunes of 'handle', flirting with over-grown schoolboys or young men... or she may seek social pleasure in the attractive pubs and drink 'four-ale' out of the same quart-pot as her 'young man'.*

*The cheap and low-class music-hall is, however, her favourite place of patronage. A threepenny seat in the top gallery with her male admirer, a paperful of fried fish and potatoes, and a bottle of ginger-beer are to her a luxury which makes her forget her poverty and life of unremunerative toil. The coarse songs and suggestive jokes are all in harmony with her life and circumstances.*

From the 1890s until WW1 lads and lasses obeyed the code of what was termed the 'monkey rank' and would gather at locations like Manchester's Oldham Street:

*Girls resort to Oldham Street on a Saturday in nearly as large numbers as the boys... The boys exchange rough salutations with the girls, who seem in no way less vigorous than the boys themselves, and whose chief desire, one would think, was to pluck from the lads' buttonholes, the flowers which many of them wear.*

## TEA, TRIPE AND TROTTERS

Not only were girls able to afford a drop of drink, there was a more varied selection in the food departments. Early in the nineteenth century most people got by on a very basic diet but later shellfish, pea soup, meat puddings, nuts, oranges, fruit pies and saveloys were washed down with tea, coffee and cocoa. Lancashire claims to have given birth to chippies, tripe and cowheel shops. Sheep's trotters were a speciality in Liverpool.

Young mothers have always been attacked by their elders, who have always "known better". A 1904 report issued by the sinisterly named 'Physical Deterioration Committee' (would they have been disbanded if they'd discovered good news?) stated:

*Girls have not the slightest sense of duty. It is only pleasure and amusement with them. The last thing they think of is duty and therefore they do not take the trouble to cook or get up in the morning, and the children go to school without breakfast*

How little times have changed.

The following report also dates from 1904:

*Many growing girls are disinclined to eat a hearty breakfast, and the majority spend their dinner-money unprofitably, choosing tarts, buns and ginger-beer to more nourishing food. Even where special restaurants are provided and hot meat and vegetables can be obtained for 3d. or 4d., a large number of girls prefer to spend an equal sum in cakes or tarts… Among the poorest girls hard work and impaired physique combine to produce a jaded appetite which craves for highly flavoured and 'tasty' food, and is a great temptation to take intoxicants.*

It appears that today's appetite for a few bevvies and a balti is not so new.

A Bolton woman from one of the better off working class families remembered her diet in the early years of the twentieth century. A typical day's breakfast of porridge and water was followed by a dinner of pea soup or hot pot made with black puddings. Tea would consist of treacle or jam butties, or sugar on bread.

Meat was usually only served on Sundays, not a chicken or a leg of lamb, but heart, which you – *'ad to eat… even if you didn't really like it…* When times were hard turnips would increasingly appear on the dinner plate.

A typical working girl's breakfast (at least for those who didn't sneak off to the cake shop) would consist of two or three slices of bread and butter (sometimes lard and dripping were substituted) and two cups of tea. The evening meal sometimes included meat but only the cheaper cuts, such as liver – with or without gravy; chitterlings (pig's small intestines), pig's fry or 'inside of pig'.

Some women's diet was a lot simpler. Margaret Canavan from 12, Townsend Street, Liverpool had

25. Potato pickers near Chorley. School was skipped if help needed on the land.

just one item on her shopping list – rum. In 1887, at the age of 45 she took to her bed and sent out for her diet of Tom Thumb. Ignoring the doctor's warnings she survived for six weeks before her inevitable demise at 7 o'clock one Saturday morning. The death certificate stated the causes as being consumption aggravated by chronic drunkenness.

Margaret's funeral was certainly a rum do. Her husband, who had been on the bottle since her death – though whether from mirth or mourning no-one could tell – entirely overlooked the necessity of arranging the burial.

Unlike Margaret, the majority of women kept up appearances. Old photos often show the pride taken in cleaning doorsteps, the time consumed being justified by the very common expression 'There's more passes by than comes in.'

26. Wright and Turners cotton mill workers

## TWO TO THE LOO

A woman, born in Halliwell in 1899, remembers using buckets as toilets. Men known as 'midnight mechanics' or 'muck misers' or 'pilgrims of the night' used to come after dark and empty them into carts, leaving a trail of sprinkled lime behind. In most homes in places like Rochdale, even as late as 1896, wooden pails made from petroleum casks cut in two were common toilet pans. Indeed the tradition of women visiting lavatories in pairs goes back a long way. In mid-Victorian Manchester the little girls' room often had no doors and it was customary for one lass to squat while another spread her coat to screen her.

Most patients admitted to hospital were so unused to flushing loos that in 1908 the Manchester Royal Infirmary experimented with WCs that flushed automatically when the door was closed on leaving. They never worked.

Given slum conditions, lack of privacy and problems with water supply, it was hard to keep clean, though most succeeded. In Preston, shortly before WW1, a mother of 13 used to bathe her children in the street in a dolly-tub. Wandering from house to house she begged for buckets of hot water and scrubbed her offspring one after the other in the same solution. This was also used for the 'washing' of clothes which her children had to put back on wet, they having no change of apparel.

In taped reminiscences, stored at Lancaster University and in Clitheroe, Lancashire lasses remember their early encounters, both with scrubbing brush and the cleanliness-is-next-to-godliness brigade. In the years leading up to WW1, teachers in Lancaster were of the belief that the most important discipline a child could learn was that of cleanliness.

One Bolton woman knelt down every night and had her hair combed for vermin and then plaited by her mother. She wore clogs and thick black stockings to school where they were thoroughly inspected *They used to look behind your ears... Those found dirty got the stick.*

In wasn't just grime that upset the cleanliness police, hand-me-downs had the same effect, as one victim recollected:

*They used to show you up if you were poor. My mother once waited a week for a teacher to give her* (the teacher) *a good hiding. We'd to wear all my mother's clothes and this teacher had pulled my sister and swung her round with her hair.*

27. *'There's more passes by than comes in.'*

## DOLLY-TUBS AND DIDDY MEN

Women did nearly all the housework and, with large families, the most onerous chore was probably the weekly wash. Clothes would be soaked the previous evening in a large dolly-tub. Early next morning a boiler would be lit and the garments vigorously rotated with a dolly. Women in an advanced state of pregnancy had to be particularly careful as it was believed this agitation might cause miscarriage. 'Whites' were followed by coloureds and heavily soiled clothes. They would be boiled for roughly half an hour, rinsed and starched. When hung out to dry wives had to keep a watchful eye on the family wear lest it be lifted by clothesline thieves. The final task was pressing with a heavy iron heated either by hot coals inserted into the iron itself, of by standing the iron on the hot plate of the stove, or by an open fire.

A few 'new men', including perhaps some of Ken Dodd's relations, could be found in Salford in the first quarter of the twentieth century.

*Some wives proudly boasted that they would never allow 'the man of the house' to do a 'hand's turn'. Derisive names like 'mop rag' and 'diddy man' were used for those who did help... One quiet street in the village where several husbands dared help their wives became known in the pubs as 'Dolly Lane' or 'Bloody-good-husband street'.* (The Classic Slum by Robert Roberts).

A written resume of the contents of a tape held at the North-West Sound Archive (Clitheroe) of another Bolton woman's early oral reminiscences would be typical of the lives endured by so many. She was born in 1906:

*Got married – no money – had pink salmon for tea – fair – fat women on fair – mother used to do her washing – people came from miles to see her knickers on the line – mother took in lodgers – used orange boxes as furniture – no carpets – went playing the piano in pubs – every time had a baby moved house – story of flit – lairn lad caught them – always had a good wash before went to borrow money.*

## SOMETHING FOR THE WEEKEND

One of the few pleasures was a chinwag with the neighbours, whether it be on the doorstep, in the pub or biweekly visit to the pawn shop. All human

28. Expectant mothers were particularly careful when using a dolly as it was believed that the agitation might cause a miscarriage.

life and their belongings were there, as discovered by a reporter from the *Liverpool Review* in the 1880s:

*Very few of this continual stream of indigent humanity are either neat or clean. A stout, flabby woman, bare-headed, with two dirty-skinned unwashed infants, elbows her way up to the front, and in a rich Irish brogue begs immediate attention as her 'ould man is waiting to go out' and she is quickly accommodated with the faded black suit she pawned on the previous Monday.*

*A girl some twenty years of age, with the appearance of a street hawker, unwashed and untidy, with small check shawl, in a shrill voice, half angry half coaxingly, demands to be served at once as she is in a 'horry' and as her flashy blue stuff dress is handed to her she roundly berates those behind the counter for detaining her.*

*Several young children, apparently neglected and uncared for, frequently plead for attention with the same experienced tones and phrases as their elders, and when served they scamper off home with their bundles as though afraid of a beating for being so long.*

On Monday morning the same slatternly, thriftless looking crowd besiege the establishment, but they are now bringing their goods to be taken care of during the week and having more time on hand a running fire of conversation is kept up both before and behind the counter, and the familiarity with which one side chaffs the other betokens a friendship born of frequent intercourse.

...The great majority represent all the phases of squalid poverty amongst the poorest classes of the labouring community, though some evidently better off people were driven to this by sheer force of circumstances and they betrayed their 'freshness' by a timidity and hesitancy at once touching and pitiable.

Walter Greenwood in *There Was A Time* recalls the ruses a Mrs Boarder would get up to in Salford during the first war. She arrived as regular as clockwork every Monday morning with a tightly wrapped pair of running shoes, the spikes protruding:

30. Theresa Baker aka 'Run away Theresa' an habitual offender imprisoned for pawning duffing jewellery in Liverpool.

The usual, she said, then pushed the next transaction across.

The pawnbroker, feeling the spikes, called out: 'Running pumps, two and six.' sent the bundle sliding down the counter, then pulled towards him the next item.

This morning the pumps were pushed across, the details called out, but as the bundle went sliding along the counter, the pin became detached, the wrapping fell away and there, in all its nakedness, the bundle's guilty secret stood discovered to all in the crowded shop.

Silence. You could hear the sparrows chirping outside.

The pawnbroker, like everybody else except Mrs Boarder and her daughter Hetty, stared at the two pieces of cardboard cut to the size and shape of the running pumps' soles. 'Wild Woodbine Cigarettes' the printing said on the cardboard. Half-inch nails protruded at appropriate places, the space between the cardboard stuffed with newspaper and the whole secured with string round toe, heel and instep...

29. Ellen Webster, one of many women imprisoned for illegal pawning in Wakefield, 1884 and Salford the following year.

When the pawnbroker threatened to call the police Mrs Boarder retaliated:

*I shall have to tell 'em about all the old-age pension books and ring papers that you've got stuffed in there... I've got all the tickets remember, and when it gets in the newspapers let's see how it goes down with all them bible-punchers that go to that chapel o' yours. Get on you preaching bleeder. You. aye, and all you stand for. You'll not be happy till you've milked us dry. He made a stammering attempt at reply but she would have none of it. 'Waste no more time, man.' She jerked her thumb* toward the pledge office. *'Back in there and let's get finished'. Another thing she warned... 'if you come this lark again trying to show me up in front of everybody I'll take all my custom somewhere else.' She swept about face and forgetting that Hetty was standing behind her, tripped and stumbled over her own daughter. Recovering balance she began to slap the girl, backhand and palm across both ears. 'All your flamin' fault, not puttin' that pin in proper. That's a regular half-dollar a week gone, you faggot, you. Haven't I got enough troubles and worries on my mind.'*

A PAWNBROKER'S SHOP ON A SATURDAY NIGHT.

*31. A regular meeting venue. Most would be back again on Monday morning.*

# 'BED AND WORK ALL THE TIME'

*32. Young girls contemplate what will probably become their future place of employment.*

Most girls entered the work place at around the age of 12. Even as late as 1900 there were no female solicitors or members of the armed forces and no policewomen. Only a handful of women had graduated as doctors and vets and indeed the prime role for educated women was that of teacher. Of these, few were expected to marry.

## THE NATURE OF EMPLOYMENT NATIONALLY AT THE END OF 19TH CENTURY

| | MEN | WOMEN |
|---|---|---|
| POLICE | 44,000 | 0 |
| ARMED FORCES | 134,000 | 0 |
| BARRISTER, SOLICITOR | 23,000 | 0 |
| VET | 3,000 | 3 |
| ACCOUNTANT | 9,000 | 50 |
| MEDICAL PRACTITIONER | 21,000 | 113 |
| AUTHOR, WRITER, JOURNALIST | 5,500 | 689 |
| GENERAL LABOURER | 659,000 | 3,000 |
| COAL MINE LABOURER | 587,000 | 3,800 |
| NATIONAL GOVERNMENT | 88,000 | 11,000 |
| NURSE, MIDWIFE ETC | 650 | 58,000 |
| FARMING | 1,043,000 | 74,000 |
| TEACHER | 57,000 | 157,000 |
| MILLINER, DRESSMAKER,TAILOR ETC | 145,000 | 566,000 |
| DOMESTIC HOUSEKEEPER, CLEANER | 123,000 | 1,600,000 |

Mothers who stayed at home faced lives of unremitting poverty, entirely dependent on the salaries of husbands who were either less than reliably employed or far from reliable providers. For men it was simply a case of in and out of work and in and out of the pub.

Most women listed their profession as 'married', but in Lancashire there were opportunities for married women to work outside the home in either the mining or cotton industries. Such work, however, brought its own hardship, for industrial conditions were, to say the least, extremely harsh.

## PIT BROW LASSES

Whether the sub-commissioner who wrote the report below displayed his true feelings in his final sentence is open to conjecture:

*One of the most disgusting sights I have seen was that of young females, dressed like boys in trousers, crawling on all fours, with belts round their waists, and chains passing between their legs as they drew loaded wagons along mine passages... The chain passing high up between the legs of the girls, had worn large holes in their trousers, and any*

33. Women and children under ten were barred from working underground in 1842.

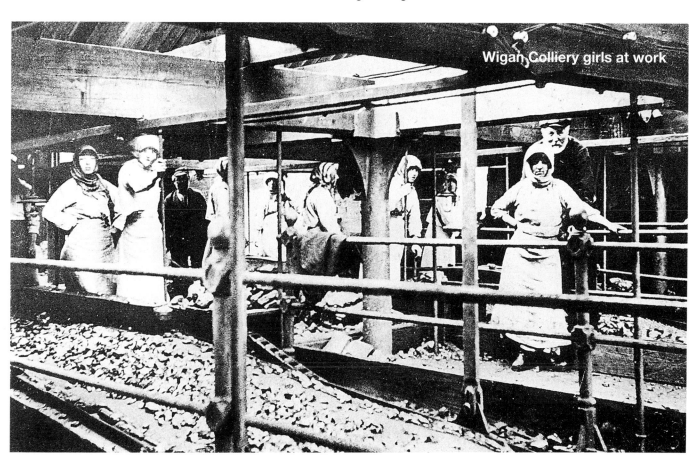

34. Most workers were single women aged between 16 and 30.

35 One in five surface workers in the 1880s was female.

*sight more disgustingly indecent or revolting can scarcely be imagined than these girls at work. No brothel can beat it.*

Prior to 1842, shocked visitors to coal mines were less concerned about semi-naked females being used as pit ponies than by the fact that women were wearing the trousers. But there was a lot more going on than met their prurient eyes.

Today we have the mile high club, but nineteenth century Lancashire miners had their equivalent 'down below'. One Wigan woman, probably unaware of the double-entendre, confided:

*I have known men take liberty with the drawers and some of the women have bastards.*

For female pit workers pregnancy and motherhood seemed almost an inconvenience, an interruption to the daily grind. Our confidante from Wigan continues:

*My clothes are wet through all day long. I never was ill in my life but when I was lying in.*

*My cousin looks after my children in the daytime. I am very tired when I get home at night. I fall asleep sometimes before I get washed. I am not so strong as I was and cannot stand my work as well as I used to. I have drawn until I have had the skin off me. The belt and chain is worse when we are in the family way. My feller has beaten me many a time for not being ready. I were not used to it at first and he had little patience. I have known many a man beat his drawer.*

Jane Harrison, an underground worker from St Helens, recollected long hours spent slaving down the mines:

*We worked three turns together, that is two days and a night. 36 hours, from 6 one morning to 6 the next night; never went to bed at all; had about an hour and a half in the 12, perhaps more, for meals. I only did so once: they don't often have to work more than 12 hours on pit brow. I believe that then it was for a ship that had to leave Liverpool sooner than they thought, and wanted coaling at once.*

WRAGG.

*36. Wigan pit brow lasses were amongst the very few women in Victorian times to wear trousers.*

By 1842 women (and children under 10) were banned from working down the mines. This decision followed a report which, unusually, contained illustrations of the working conditions. From that date, women and girls worked on the surface and became known as 'pit brow lasses'.

## FINE HEALTHY WENCHES

In 1910, one of the most remarkable of Victorian diarists left instructions that three boxes of photographs, drawings and notes should not be opened until forty years after his death. In 1950 the poet and barrister's boxes were dusted down and a remarkable collection of illustrations and reminiscences were sifted through at Trinity College, Cambridge.

The diarist was one A.J. Munby. An eccentric who had secretly married a maidservant, Munby was a regular visitor to the coalfields of Wigan. An enthusiast for women labourers, the dirtier the better, Munby described the pits near Wigan as *the picturesque headquarters of rough female labour*. As the following extracts illustrate, he seemed to really enjoy his excursions up north:

### HINDLEY 1859

*Those black nondescript creatures pushing the waggons along the embankments would not be noticed by travellers on the line; they would pass for men: but I recognised them at once as my stout hearty friends, the Lancashire colliergirls. The costume of these girls and women is always the same, and a good useful one it is. A hooded bonnet of padded cotton, pink blue or black: a blue striped shirt, open at the breast, a waistcoat of cloth, generally double-breasted but ragged and patched throughout: fustian or corduroy or sometimes blackcloth trousers, patched with all possible materials except the original one, and stout clog shoon, brassclasped on their bare feet: round the waist is clasped a petticoat of striped cotton, blue and black, rolled up as a joiner rolls his apron: it is never let down, and is perfectly useless only retained as a symbol of sex*

### IN A COLLIER'S HOUSE NEAR WIGAN, 1860

*...the door was driven open, and in burst the two wenches, Ellen Meggison and Jane, shouting and*

37. Photographs or 'cartes' of the girls in both fashionable dresses and their work clothes became extremely popular in Victorian Lancashire.

*tumbling over one another like lads at a fair. They were both of course in their pitclothes, and as black as ever; and their grimy faces were bathed in sweat, for they had been running home all the way. The mother began to rate Jane soundly for staying at the alehouse and being out so late (it was now 7.30).*

*'Is that the way for a respectable woman?' thundered she. The girls shouted in reply that they had had to do overwork and to wait for their wages; and the hubbub subsided... Jane sat down to her supper of Irish stew; scooping the potatoes out of the bowl with a leaden spoon, and holding the meat in her black fingers while she tore it from the bone with her teeth.*

*Her mother and I meanwhile stood and looked at her – she eating away unconcerned and hungry – and remarked what a fine healthy wench she was, and how she was not seventeen till next month, and so on. And yet this colliergirl of seventeen is ten times more robust and womanly than her elder sister the factory girl.*

*38. The studio photos romanticised a job that was dull and back-breaking.*

## MARCH 1865, MET POINTSWOMAN

*Her name was Margaret Roughley and her age 17. This Margaret was a wellgrown girl: her collier bonnet was tilted over her eyes, which sparkled under lashes thickly clogged with coal dust; her face was very black, but also singularly expressive and intelligent; her arms were bare; she had a woollen comforter round her neck; a loose patched shirt, looking very thin and cold; a short baglike apron of sackcloth; short fustian trousers, only reaching to the calf; grey stockings, and big clog shoon, whose iron soles were turned up at the toe like a chinaman's boot. Had she no coat? I asked: it must be very cold waiting about in this cutting all day, No, she had not: but the Gaffer's very kind – he lends me his coat when it rains: and besides, she said. Aw don't stop here all day; Aw'us waggons to fill wi' slack; 20 waggons a day sometimes; yo'd not think it was idling if yo'd got that to do! And Margaret laughed a boyish laugh, and showed her white teeth, like Irish diamonds set in black bog oak.*

Munby later conversed with a woman who worked in the mines in 1849, seven years after they had been banned:

*A woman in peacoat and fustian trousers came out of the engine house in a leisurely manner, her hands in her pockets. She had a very striking face; aquiline features, a strong jaw and a bold chin, and hazel eyes so large and keen that to meet their gaze was like breasting the blow of a mountain breeze. She said she was 37 years old, but looked nearly ten years younger: she was strong and square-built, but not coarse nor large. And who was this beauty, whose face begrimed as it was, was so handsome and powerful and expressive? Why, she was a mere quadruped. She had been brought up in service but of her own accord had left that calling, about fifteen years ago, to work as a drawer. Of course she went as a man; but she liked it. and liked the work. Did she draw with the belt and chain? 'Yes', she said: 'I was harnessed to the corves, with the belt around my body and the chain between my legs, hooked on to the corves.' And did not the harness hurt you? 'No, my breeches kept the chain from hurting my legs.' And you went on your hands and feet, just as a horse goes on four legs. 'Yes, just the same' she said simply. 'and the roads was rough – there was no rails when I draw'd: it was over my wrists in mud. often. I used to draw the corves 200 or 300 yards; I could do it easily. I don't mind going on my hands*

*and feet for that distance and more; oh no! And it did not make my hands very hard, using them as if they was feet; nor harder than they are now'. 'I liked it' she said with emphasis: 'but when I'd been working down a month, they found out I was a woman, and I was turned out: and since then I've worked on pit-brow and worn breeches, as I'm doing now.'*

## CANOODLING IN THE CARDROOMS

Although work in the mills paid fairly well, they were not particularly pleasant places because of the incessant clanking of dangerous machinery, variations of temperature and poor facilities.

In mills with several floors the toilets were often closets with a large hole, the excreta falling down a shaft to a communal cesspool at the bottom. No ashes were used, and, as may be imagined, *a most offensive odour* was given off. A report from the medical officer of health in Preston summed up the problem. There was certainly little incentive to slip out for a swift ciggy or chinwag:

39. One reporter commented: 'At about 30 [mill workers] seem to collapse in one shrinking, wrinkling fall, from girls to old women.'

40. Accidents were common as machines were rarely turned off.

*The closets themselves are so small, confined and badly ventilated, that each person during the time of using them is exposed to the foul gasses from the cesspool below, and this, very often, when from the high temperature of the workroom just left, the body is in a heated condition, and so more liable to absorb the dangerous effluvia.*

A Bolton woman remembers conditions in the early 1900s:

*In those days they never stopped the machinery while you cleaned it, you had to clean it running… Nelly Storey got her fingers fast in a wiper, taken under the wheels. Her fingers were ripped off on the wiper and the machine shut. It pulled her hand down and the wiper was still there with her fingers on. They took her to the welfare. Some fool poured iodine on the stumps. She was demented. Well, when the ambulance came the men went mad. They said 'it's a wonder she's not gone off her rocker'.*

Another worker remembers the machines in the cardrooms being particularly dangerous:

*The girl who trained me, she was scalped by one of them. She got it fast in a machine. They used to put machines on the cards, and it was running and she caught her hair in it and it scalped her. It pulled her hair out. After that she always had very thin, straggly hair.*

Because of the harsh conditions in the mills women began to lose their looks earlier than in other jobs. One unkind male observer generalised, *at about 30 [mill workers] seem to collapse in one shrinking, wrinkling fall, from girls to old women.*

It's often argued that education only begins when schooldays are over. In the milltowns girls would often work part-time at school and part-time in the cotton industry. They may have learnt more arithmetic at school but the mill was the place for multiplication.

Margaret McCarthy, who later became a militant left-wing activist and Labour M.P., was born in Oswaldtwistle in 1911. Her first days as a 12-year-old half-time cotton weaver certainly opened her eyes:

*Two women and one man, employed in our small corner of a large, dark warehouse, behaved in a singular fashion. The man, although married, was apparently the lover of one of the women and they made very little effort to conceal the fact. From where I sat all day, desperately separating the cotton strands and thrusting them on the drawer's ever-waiting hooks, I could see him fondling her, hands deep within her blouse or beneath her petticoats.*

*The thick, blurred, excited tones which the voice of the other woman took on, when the man was alone with her, led me to feel that something similar was happening in her case, although her machine was too far away for me to have seen anything.*

41. Workers leaving Melbourne Mill, Accrington c1910. Winders and warpers considered themselves a class above the weavers and dressed accordingly.

## CHOPPING CHIPS AND GRINDING SANDSTONE

Those not employed in service, in the mills or pits had to make ends meet the best they could. Poverty seemed to be around every Liverpool street corner. In the courts of Vauxhall ward:

*...traces of sandstone or chips may be noticed on the ground. Amongst those women it is wonderful that so much womanhood survives the labour of draught horses and the lives of savages. As they kneel or squat, splitting their chips or pulverising their sandstone, with their well-oiled hair, short petticoats and muscular limbs, it is possible to trace in some of them touches of native beauty of which many a fine lady might be proud.*

(Liverpool Review).

One year later the *Liverpool Citizen* complained that doing 'men's work' brutalised women.

*Gangs of girls stroll through the streets whose language is utterly unfit for the ears of passers-by. All the savagery that lies dormant in our species seems to be roused into maddening excitement under the evil influences which surround these women and girls in the circumstances of their every day lives.*

*Let us look into one of these warehouses where women are working at rags, cotton or refuse. The room is close, the work is hard and the words are wilfully obscene. What is slangily termed a 'tarpaulin mister' is made for drink. A jug or can is borrowed, or perhaps the whole party adjourns en masse to the too familiar counter at the corner where the saddening spectacle is seen of women who are mothers, and girls who will ere long be mothers, standing side by side taking their turn in emptying the glasses which will soon be filled again.*

Take the Lancashire coalfields for example where the coarse, hard, ingrained nature of the working classes is proverbial. Yet it is in these very districts where women work at tasks altogether unsuitable to their weaker mental and muscular fibre, that the coarseness reaches its maximum. The sacred ties of the family, the moral relations of the sexes, are sapped by the exposure of the woman to the wearying work of the man. In the working population of the brickfields and the floating life on the canals the same sad symptoms of moral degradation, brought on by degrading influences are plainly perceptible.

Here in Liverpool, the climax of immorality, drunkenness and disease appears to be attained. The wrecked homes, the ruined family ties, the wretched waifs, offsprings of the offenders against the 'moral law' are visible to the most superficial observer.

## HOMEWORKERS ON FIVE SHILLINGS A WEEK

Possibly the lowest paid workers were women who contracted to do piece work at home. In the 1880s the price for the rent of a sewing machine was two shillings and sixpence a week, and, even working twelve hour shifts, many women struggled to turn out shirts, trousers and waistcoats which would earn them much more than five shillings weekly.

A reporter in Liverpool visited a home in which both mother and daughter had been widowed. They worked extremely long hours at slave labour rates to help keep a little food in the bellies of the three emaciated children. Those in a similar position were known as the 'slop workers of Liverpool'. Let's listen in to some of the conversation with the mother:

42. Fish saleswoman, Wigan.

43. Boatwomen were generally poorly educated and often before the courts for brawling.

– Is the making of waistcoats the worst paid work?

– No, trousers are worse than waistcoats. At the shop they only pay 5d. for making a pair of trousers, and you have to find your own thread out of that. That would make about 4d. for the work.

– Could a woman make two pairs of trousers in a day?

– She might do it but she would have to do with very little sleep. Then when they work at night there's light to be paid for, and a bit of fire if they can manage it so that you really don't earn much more by working long hours.

– Do many women take this work at such a rate of payment?

– I know one woman who refused it this morning, but most of them can't help themselves. They just have to take whatever's offered to them.

Leaving her daughter slaving over the sewing machine, the mother would seek out more lucrative work:

– I go out 'charing' when I can get a job, and I'm paid 2s. a day and my food. To do that I have to work from eight o'clock in the morning until ten or eleven at night, and at my age I'm not so strong that I don't feel it. But I would be only too glad if I could get the chance of doing it oftener.

– Then the fact is, if you could go out every day, and had strength for the work, you could earn 12s. a week clear as a charwoman, while your daughter can't earn 5s. a week at the cheap shops, and has to find food out of that?

– Yes; if I had the strength to do it, but I haven't. I do the best I can.

## THE RAG TRADE

Rag and cotton pickers had some of the dirtiest factory jobs, sifting through old, often soiled clothing, the refuse of industrial tailors and dressmakers. They had to quickly and nimbly separate the rags from a mixed heap into categories such as 'common softs' 'whites' 'seconds' 'thirds' etc. Rag-pickers earned about 1s 4d per day for ten hours work.

Cotton-pickers earned between five and seven shillings a week and had to put in a full twelve hour shift. The most arduous part of the job was working in the drying room used to repair damaged cotton. Here a tiled floor covered a number of steam pipes, making the room extremely uncomfortable. Let's join a *Liverpool Review* reporter who, in 1901, experienced a few minutes of the kinds of working conditions endured by rag pickers.

*The women's business is to spread the bales over this floor, and about every half-hour go into the room, damp the cotton and turn it. The process is very much like that of turning hay, but instead of working in the bright sunshine and fresh air, the cotton-pickers work in a hot room, the temperature of which resembles that in the hottest room in a Turkish bath. In some cases it is hotter. The excessive heat, combined with the unpleasant effluvia of steaming, damp cotton, is of course conductive to ill-health and disease. Very often the weaker and less experienced cotton-pickers are carried out of the hot room in a fainting condition.*

## TAKEN TO THE CLEANERS

Laundry workers were divided into three categories: washers, starchers and ironers. All three classes worked twelve hour shifts commencing at eight o'clock in the morning. One and a half hours were set aside for meal breaks.

Washers and starchers were paid between 9s. and 15s. weekly. Ironers were on piece work and would earn 2d. a dozen for collars and 1s. 3d. a dozen for shirts. This was a comparatively well-paid job but it must be remembered that the iron weighed about 4lbs. Saturday was the big day for the laundries with many women having to work to the early hours of Sunday morning. Monday afternoon was given in lieu. Time to do their own washing?

## STANDING ONLY

Several young shop workers lived in and were provided with some food and laundry but even those who didn't were expected to work long shifts, sometimes 12-14 hours a day. Writing of life in 1900's Manchester, Stella Davies, in her book *North Country Bred*, remembers her 17-year-old sister returning on Saturday nights from her job at Lewis's department store.

*[She] would arrive home at nearly midnight, having walked the mile from the tram to our house and after having been on her feet all the long day (shop assistants were not allowed to sit down in view of customers), exhausted to breaking point. She would weep with weariness and although hungry be too tired to eat her supper. She would perk up a bit on Sunday but obviously dreaded the return to work on Monday.*

**WOMEN'S WAGES 1902**

| | |
|---|---|
| GENERAL SERVANTS AND SCULLERY MAIDS | £8 to £20 p.a. |
| KITCHEN MAIDS UNDER NURSES | £10 to £18 p.a. |
| HOUSEMAIDS | £14 to £25 p.a. |
| PARLOUR MAIDS AND LADIES MAIDS | £18 to £30 p.a. |
| COOKS, COOK HOUSEKEEPERS | £30 to £60 p.a. |
| SHOP GIRL (LIVING IN) | £10 to £60 p.a. |
| SHOP GIRL (LIVING OUT) | up to £100 p.a. |
| BARMAIDS (hours 14 to 18 daily) | 10 - 15 shillings p.w. |
| WAITRESSES (hours 9 to 11) | 9 - 12 shillings p.w. |
| INFERIOR TYPISTS (hours 8) | 10 - 15 shillings p.w. |
| CAPABLE BUSINESS CLERK (hours 8) | 20 - 35 shillings p.w. |
| TELEGRAPHISTS (HOURS 8) | 10 - 28 shillings p.w. |

*44. With new technology came new jobs. Telegram deliverer in the Oldham area.*

45. *Cockling at Morecambe Bay. The local clergyman was outraged at the behaviour of the younger worker: 'Taking the eight or nine villages on the shores of Morecambe Bay there must be several hundreds of children who, owing to the cockling business are growing up in a state of heathenism.*

## THE 'HEATHENS' OF MORECAMBE BAY

Not all work was sweated labour in slumland. In the Morecambe Bay area many mothers and daughters were employed in the cockling industry. Armed with three-pronged bent forks, gangs of workers spent hours bent almost double digging up the shellfish hiding just one inch below the surface. The exposure to bracing sea winds was considered worthwhile when the harvest was good and promised – with the help of all the children – earnings as much as £4 per week.

Like most employment in Victorian times, cockling did, however, have its downside. A Mrs Butler of Flookborough remembers how her three daughters were:

*Generally absent from home ten or twelve hours together; in spring tides they have to walk five miles to the banks, which, with a mile to the shore, makes twelve miles going and returning, besides cockling for five hours. They are a bit tired when they come home, and are quite ready for a meal; they have nothing on the sands but a piece of bread, of which they eat a little now and then just to keep off hunger. It is a slavish life but what are poor people to do? My girls went to the infant school until they were eight, but they have not been to any school since; they cannot read.*

## THE EYE OF THE BEHOLDER?

In a society so paranoid about sex that piano legs were sometimes covered lest they excite unwonted attention, even a country town like Flookborough had its own moral guardian. The Right Reverend T. Rigg believed that, at the first opportunity, the girls and boys of rural parts, when left to their own devices, would fall into competition with rabbits. He was particularly offended by working women's habits of tucking their long dresses between their legs and leaving the lower limbs exposed. He also objected to the coarse language and lifestyle of many of his cockling neighbours:

*The children and young persons engaged in this business are in a very demoralized condition; they never enter a place of worship, and their language when idling about the streets is disgusting. At 14 boys and girls become so independent that they often leave their parents and lodge with strangers, spending their earnings in drunkenness, even at that early age... Taking the eight or nine villages on the shores of Morecambe Bay there must be several hundreds of children who, owing to this cockling business, are growing up in a state of heathenism. Quite as much necessity exists for putting this system under regulation as in the agricultural gangs of which I have read. Boys, girls, young men, and women are out for hours together on the sands without the slightest control, and the results to morality may be imagined.*

46. Coal picking near Chorley.

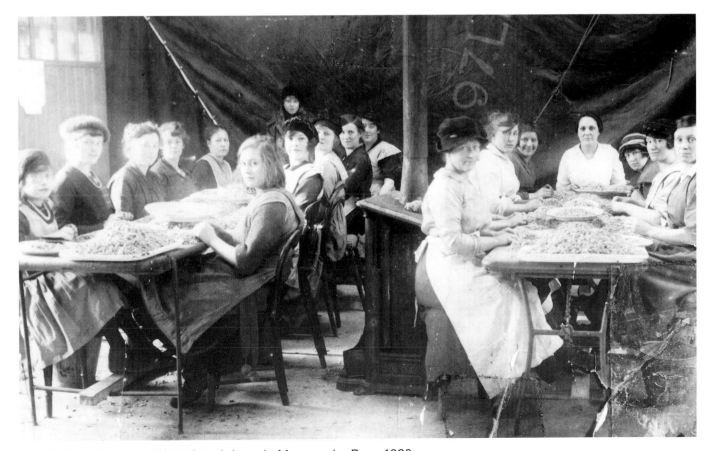

47. Picking, shelling and bagging shrimps in Morecambe Bay c1920.

## LADIES OF THE NIGHT

Instead of concerning himself with the innocent cocklers from Morecambe, the Reverend Rigg might have been better advised attending to the needs of the ubiquitous Lancashire street walkers.

Rather than endure the crude conditions of sweat shops, mines and mills, many young ladies took up the world's oldest profession. In 1866, another Victorian man of the cloth questioned girls as to why they had chosen to walk the streets in Oldham. He published the following details of his interviewees:

| Age | Years of Service | Reason for Choice |
|---|---|---|
| 36 | 13 | seduced by overlooker at mill in Ashton |
| 25 | 4 | want of employment |
| 26 | 7 | 'sheer wickedness' |
| 29 | 7 | seduced by sweetheart |
| 25 | 7 | seduced by overlooker at mill in Ashton |
| 22 | 1 | servant in pub seduced by traveller |
| 25 | 3 | want of employment |
| 25 | 7 | seduced by overlooker at mill in Ashton |
| 25 | 7 | servant in pub, commenced through drunkenness |
| 22 | 6 | servant in pub, commenced through drunkenness |
| 20 | 1 | seduced by employer at mill |
| 25 | 7 | seduced by manager of mill |

48. Sarah Files, a Rochdale sex worker and drinker. Six months for various drunken offences.

It appears that the overlooker at the mill in Ashton was not content with merely looking over and was something of a ladies' man. Whether he attracted the girls by carrot or stick (threats of the sack?) only he and they knew.

How did girls become street walkers? In an article for the *Social Gazette* in 1898 the reporter argues that probably the main reasons lasses sold their bodies were unemployment and poverty. Below he describes the path from loss of work to prostitution:

*They roam the streets or trudge to poorly-paid work in thin clothes and thinner boots: they sleep in crowded rooms, live on bread and cheese, sausage and pickles, work long hours in factory or shop… A situation is lost for one or many varying reasons and lo! at the end of a few weeks the Grey Wolf peers around the little top back-room door.*

*What can a friendless girl do then? The rent must be paid. When homelessness looms near, the very look of the streets at night makes one shiver. Then the pawnshop comes in a vision, and the Grey Wolf draws a single step backward as the girl comes up the stair with the pawning price of the only little trinket in her hand.*

49. Another Rochdale lass. 50-year-old Catherine Day. One month for frequenting, 1895.

*After that? Oh after that is the careful eking out of slices of the loaf and dinners, made up of penny packets of soup, cooked over a few sticks from the halfpenny bundle, brought in under the cloak, from the little general shop at the corner… And there are the temptations and offers that are insults to be borne – the leering, well-fed ghouls who prevent the eyes from gladdening themselves with a feast of fancy at the shop-windows. Men who note the anxious glance and throb in the voice that asks for employment, and who say. 'Well, I'm very sorry – the situation's filled. I'm afraid you'll find it a hard matter to get a place now: everything is overcrowded. But _____ .*

*Sometimes the loneliness and the hunger are too great for a girl's tender heart, and the blank is filled with the harlot's soul. Now and then the river carries out to sea a young woman who thought its dark waters better than the awful, mocking, pitiless lighted town…*

Some help was at hand in larger towns for those seeking to escape the life. Homes, like the Midnight Mission in Everton, were set up where girls might stay for an average of twenty weeks. Here survivors of the street would be trained in laundry and needlework with the hope that they would eventually find legitimate employment. Was it really possible for girls to give up the game and go into the legalised slavery that was factory work and domestic service? Even reporters of the time doubted it.

After observing a twenty-year-old prostitute being sent to a care home for three months rather than to prison, Robert Blatchford wrote from the Manchester courts:

*If the society preach at this girl, harp too much upon her iniquity, try to make her religious, bid her wear drab frocks, brush her hair flat, and become respectable, I fear the attempt will fail. The girl is young and full of life; she is vain, fickle, fond of finery and pleasure; has all the characteristics of a society young lady; all the craving for excitement, all the coquetry and zest for admiration. You cannot make such metal into patient Grissels. This kind of woman cannot brook the slavery of the maid-of-all-work, or the sweater's seamstress; it is very wicked of her, of course, but _____ !*

The chairman of the care home accepted that where there is demand there will always be supply but defended his institution with the argument that the supply often produced the demand.

*50. 26-year-old sex worker Mary Jane Taylor was convicted three times in Rochdale.*

*51. 22-year-old Henrietta Whitehead's profession was listed on police files as 'prostitute'. Sent down for one month for stealing £4. 17s.*

52. As a port Liverpool provided rich but dangerous pickings for sex workers.

**FROM SHAME TO SERVICE.**

53. And back again?

The official number of women 'living in shame' in Liverpool in 1884 was 1,200. These were assembled in 450 brothels. Their numbers were swollen by part-time and casual sex-workers drawn from other, poorly paying professions.

The police attitude to street walkers varied from town to town and city to city. Relations were good in Preston. A woman whose brother, Jock, was in the force remembers the stories he told of the times just after WW1.

The local pick-up was the Balmoral pub (known locally as the Bad Moral). Here the girls would come tumbling out of the ale-house after downing a concoction of drinks topped up with methylated spirits. *They would come out fighting anybody as would look at them.* The good neighbourhood cop, Jock, knew all the locals and would say *Oh, it's Lizzie! Come on, pick her up and take her to her room in the lodging house.* Here Lizzie was *thrown onto the bed* to sleep off the effects of her over-indulgence. The following day she would sing Jock's praises for having taken her home rather than to the police cell. Jock was a gentleman who treated everybody equally before the law.

*Well we knew the prostitutes and they are some of the grandest lasses you could wish for.*

The admiration appeared to be mutual with the girls repaying the compliment *The best policeman on the force!* They would greet him with cries of *How are you Jock?*

# 'THERE IS NO HEAVEN BUT WOMEN, NOR NO HELL SAVE MARRIAGE'

*THOMAS WEBBE (1660s)*

## BROKEN PROMISES AND HONEYED WORDS

There was nothing more titillating in Victorian courtrooms and newspapers than a good 'breach of promise to marry' case. Actions were brought against the moneyed classes and extensively reported in local rags for the entertainment of all bar the unhappy participants.

A typical case was played out at Manchester Assizes in 1884 when Jane Davies, formerly a barmaid at the Ship Hotel, Bradshawgate, Bolton sought damages of £1,000. She claimed that a trainee vet named Cranmer had promised to tie the knot with her and subsequently married someone else. The accused, not in court, was represented by a top lawyer who argued that, at the time of the engagement, his client was under twenty-one and therefore not liable for his actions.

In her evidence, Jane, now 22, and described as *attractive looking*, told the court that she and Cranmer met in a pub and had swiftly fallen for each other. Whether this was before, or after, Cranmer informed her that he was to inherit seven thousand pounds on his birthday, was not revealed.

Jane accepted his proposal and the couple were officially engaged. Discussing a destination for the honeymoon, Jane suggested North Wales or Paris. At the time Cranmer was under twenty-one but the relationship continued after he received the key to the door. It was a rather strange affair as the young beau bombarded his sweetheart with letters which he would personally deliver. Like a fixated lapdog he never took his eyes from hers as his beloved eagerly devoured his honeyed words. Only two of the letters remained and were read out in court. For some reason he addressed the first letter to Mary, not Jane:

*My own Dear Mary,*
*I shall be going to Blackpool for a fortnight with my sister, so I can then look for a nice house. I shall have plenty of time to get a good one if you will tell me what part you would like to live in. I will leave it entirely to you; at the same time we shan't want it until we come back from the continent. I am longing for the time to come, but it's not long to wait. You will perhaps say that when I am at Blackpool I shall see someone I like better but I shan't. For you I have been longing and now I have won you nothing on my part shall come between us and separate us. I tell you openly and candidly I do really love you and no other. I ask you the same question, do you love me? Do tell me and I shall always be your own.*

CRANMER

Jane did not have to resort to the pen as the postman/writer stood imploringly before her. She answered with a kiss. The second letter was delivered, once again by hand, a couple of weeks later. Here Cranmer, now twenty-one, addresses Jane by another name:

*Dear Polly,*
*The time is very short, it is only about three weeks and then I hope we shall take on ourselves that serious ceremony. I say serious because it is not for a day but for a lifetime. I have thought very much about it, and also of you, but you did not know that I confess to you (which it is my duty to) that as a boy fresh from school I have been a flirt, but at the same time, since I have known you, I have always thought that when you are married I shall be happy to the end with you. I shall do my best to please you and make you happy and comfortable. There shall be nothing wanting. I have given you my love; all I ask is, have you given me yours? If so, then I am 'happy as the day am long' as the darkie said. Mr and Mrs R are agreeable, so what could we wish for more? Answer me that one question and then I shall be happy. Au revoir – your only'*

CRANMER

*P.S. Kisses are reserved for future date.*

There were obviously some advantages of dispensing with the postman, the couple fell into a deep embrace.

Cranmer's attorney could not dispute the facts so he sought to discredit the would-be bride. His questioning sought to suggest that she did not really love his client and may have been a gold-digger:

– *Did he never complain that you were cold to him, and that you would not be alone with him if you could help it?*
– *No, he never complained of that.*
– *You did not like him to kiss you?*
– *Not when anybody was about.*
– *But he did not often see you when nobody was about.*
– *Yes he did.*
– *Are you engaged to be married now?*
– *No, I am not.*
– *Have you had offers of marriage during your engagement with him?*
– *Yes.*
– *And have you refused because of that engagement?*
– *Yes.*

With no witnesses being called by the defence, and the accused having admitted he had promised to marry Jane, all that remained to be resolved was the amount of compensation. When asked by the judge whether Cranmer was employed in anything his counsel's reply brought about much laughter in court:

*No, he does nothing, he is only a gentleman.*

Damages of £250 were awarded.

## THE QUEEN OF HEARTS

With such high stakes to be won many women with rather dubious claims chanced their arm in the courts. In Manchester, 1883, Mary Duke Cox, described as a barmaid in a principle restaurant, bought an action against her former employer, a Mr Lee, for breach of promise of marriage. Mr Lee's sole defence was simply that he had never proposed.

Mary would not have appreciated the reporter's comment that she looked a lot older than the thirty three years she owned up to. Seeking £1,000 compensation, Mary came across as a hard-headed and determined woman, dare we say a gold-digger, who gave her evidence in an unemotional business-like manner.

The couple met three years previously, and, according to Mary, Mr Lee proposed marriage one year later. There was just one condition. She had to agree to his being the only man who came to visit her in her Ducie Street apartment. He promised: *If you do that and keep yourself devoted to me, I will marry you.*

Mary adopted an apparently monogamous lifestyle. The couple swapped presents. He gave her broaches and 'a few trifling things'. She lent him money and made presents of jewellery and a dozen pairs of socks which she knitted herself.

With the possibility of losing such a large amount of money, Mr Lee engaged professional counsel who set about a little muck raking. His representative began to question her about her 'immoral' life and her previous male visitors. She denied ever having eight male visitors in one night but did admit to seeing six. Mary attested that when men called upon her she would ask them what they would have. They were, she said, just friends who dropped in to visit her and usually opted to drink champagne. When the bubbly was exhausted they would down gin, brandy, rum and whisky and play 'nap' until the early hours of the morning.

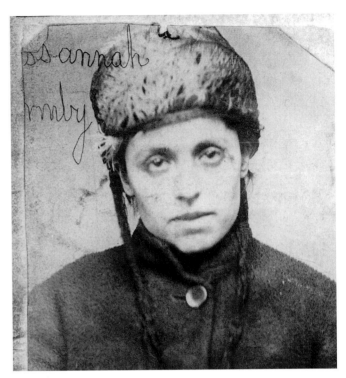

54. Susannah Formby 'forgot' she was married. Sent down for one month for bigamy.

The outraged judge had already made up his own mind. He let his views be known in no uncertain terms to the jury, stating that it was the most disgraceful case he had ever heard. Instead of the £1,000 she had been seeking, Mary Duke Cox was awarded just £2. She would doubtless have to return to card evenings to supplement her income, though it's unlikely she played solo.

## MILL LASSES, MATRIMONY AND MONOTONY

Many women endured appalling marriages to brutish drunkards for economic reasons. A deserted wife was not credit worthy and, with their significantly lower earning power, making ends meet was extremely difficult for widows and unmarried women. Single girls had little choice other than to share lodgings, never to have their own home.

Economic and peer pressure to tie the knot was extremely powerful. In the 1890s the national average age of first marriage for women was 24 and life expectancy about 48. Some girls rushed into marriage when barely out of their teens. A Lancashire parson described the wedding rituals of young mill lasses in the 1880s:

*Nineteen and twenty are very usual ages for getting married and even two and three years younger are not so infrequent as they ought to be, while the pale faces and half-developed looks make* it a spectacle painful to look upon; the result being that men and women are elevated into the dignity of grandparents before they have well entered into middle-life.

Saturday is the favourite day for getting married because it is a short one, and the ceremony can be got through with a minimum of loss – a thing certain to be considered by a thrifty operative. The town is paraded for a few hours in cheap tawdry finery of glaring colours, which can never serve any useful purpose again; perhaps one of the watering places is visited if it be fine; and on Monday morning by the stroke of six the newly married couple may be found at their looms in defiance of all poetry and romance, and the wear and tear of life begin with them once more in real earnest. Marriage asks no alteration in the position of the wife so far as mill work is concerned; she puts in her ten hours a day now as she did before. Indeed she has incomparably the worst of the bargain, for when the day's work is over, it is her privilege to light the fire at home, get the supper ready, and do the necessary household work, while it is the prerogative of the husband to use his leisure according to his own sweet will.

When the time comes for the baby to be born, the mother-expectant withdraws from the mill for a few weeks, and when she is well enough to resume her place at the loom, the baby is placed in the care of some old crone, who is past work herself and ekes out sufficient to live on by taking charge of five or six of these luckless babies for the consideration of a shilling or two a week, according to the age.

55. Chilling out with a clay pipe. Couples stayed together as divorce was difficult.

The stipulations in the bargain are very exact: the child is not to be brought before six in the morning, nor remain after six at night, while the old body is relieved altogether on Sunday of her duties as deputy.

## SENT DOWN FOR THIRTY MINUTES

With divorce being so difficult and expensive, some women would 'forget' they were married, leave their partner, possibly adopt an alias and seek new lodgings, sometimes just a couple of miles from their previous home.

Probably only a small number of those entering into bigamous marriages were ever brought to court. 30-year-old Louisa Benson was one of the unlucky few. Just two days before Christmas, 1886, she had gone through a form of marriage knowing her husband to be alive. In February the following year she pleaded guilty to a charge of bigamy in the dock in Liverpool. Louisa had been arrested because her first husband had grassed on her to the police. Following one month in custody, Louisa's unblinking eyes were charged with hatred as she stared across the courtroom at the man who gave evidence against her.

Her first and legal husband admitted under oath that he had been to prison several times and never made provision for his spouse. Every time he was released he would demand the money his wife had earned to drown his sorrows in the local pub. Louisa, *a woman of very prepossessing appearance*, pleaded in mitigation that she had met Benson when she was just 17. A few days after the birth of her first child he had left her and only returned when he heard that she had found a good position. He tried to persuade her to support him. Louisa bigamously married her second husband, James May, because she wished to make a home for herself and her children and wanted protection from the drunken lazy oaf she had been enamoured with whilst little more than a child. The bully Benson threatened her every time their paths crossed.

HIS LORDSHIP: (to Benson) *And you gave your wife into custody. Can you tell me why you did so?*

HUSBAND: *Because she said she wouldn't leave me alone. I had to call two policemen to remove her, and she gave me a black eye.*

HIS LORDSHIP: *Is there truth in what she said in your presence?*

NO ANSWER

HIS LORDSHIP: (excitedly) *Do you hear what I say. Is there truth in what she says? Be careful how you answer me.*

HUSBAND: *There is some truth in it.*

HIS LORDSHIP: *Go down.*

A most extraordinary sentence was then passed, the judge imprisoning Louisa for half an hour. This sentence was so well received by the women in court that spontaneous applause broke out. This was swiftly suppressed.

## ROUGH-HOUSES IN ROCHDALE

Once tied, the knot was difficult to undo. Couples drifted apart, sometimes amicably, mostly not. Some women, realising they had made a mistake, were willing to undertake a cut in their income to rid themselves of an unwanted partner. It was not that easy. The first step was to apply for a separation order which would, in theory, rid them of their husband, and provide them with some income. It appears that married life in towns like Rochdale was not exactly love's young dream. Over the years canoodling gave way to cooking and cleaning, while flirting was frequently replaced by fisticuffs.

Details about what really went on behind closed doors were reported in the local papers in 1908. Mrs Nields, of Strange Street off Spotland – where both wives and footballs were traditionally kicked – sought a separation order from her husband on the grounds of persistent cruelty. The mother of eight children, four of whom had died in infancy, apparently gave as good as she got. Cross-examined by her husband's attorney Mrs Nields was brutally honest:

– *You have used the poker pretty often?*
– *I have no doubt I have (Laughter).*
– *Have you thrown any ornaments at defendant?*
– *No.*
– *Spoons?*
– *Yes.*
– *Tea-cups?*
– *No.*
– *Loaves of bread?*
– *Yes.*
– *All sorts of things?*
– *Not all that you mention. I shall tell no lies about it.*
– *You have abused him a good deal?*
– *I have struck him in self defence.*

– *You have some rather fancy names for him?*
– *And he has for me.*

It was here that the magistrates intervened, saying that it was a waste of time to continue with the application as it could not possibly succeed.

A similar case was played out in the same court later that year. Once again a wife, Lizzie Lockwood, was seeking separation on the grounds of cruelty and appeared in the dock with her eye blackened. On this occasion her husband was allowed to question her. After eliciting that she had struck him in the face after he had called her 'a foul name' Mr Lockwood asked:

– *Did you throw the salt cellar and pepper-box at me and hit me in the face with a 2s. piece?*
– *Yes.*
– *And I did not hit you back?*
– *No.*

The shiner was not enough evidence and once again no separation order was granted.

One such order, instigated by the husband in the same court, was successful. Craven Elgin could no longer tolerate his wife's alcoholism. The mother of six children, five under sixteen, was permanently paralytic and incapable of doing any jobs in their Sawyer Street home. Returning after a day's work, he would repeatedly find the Missis slumped in front of the fire, snoring loudly, sleeping off the drink. In the previous two years, she had not been sober for more than three consecutive days.

Mrs Elgin had resorted to pawning everything in the house to feed her habit and there were now only rags left on the beds. The children consequently had to be sent elsewhere to sleep and had no change of underwear. For his part, Craven slept in his working gear lest he too be left with nothing. He also kept a tight grip on the bedclothes, as they too had been pawned in the past.

A shoemaker in the area supported the father's case testifying that he had often seen Mrs Elgin collapsed in the streets looking like *a dirty bundle of rags.*

When asked if she was going to reform, the tall stoutly built wife stated that she had not been given a chance. Mr Elgin was granted the separation order and told to pay his wife eight shillings a week from his 38 shillings income.

# SAVAGES AND WILD, WILD WOMEN

56. *Most of the spectators and a high number of the accused were female. Most offences were drink related resulting in fines of about ten shillings or two weeks inside.*

Unceremoniously ushered into the Liverpool Bridewell the mother, clutching her two-year-old daughter determinedly to her breast, was herself tightly restrained in the clutches of a brawny 'busy'. Having earlier succumbed to the temptation of popping in for a few glasses of ale on the way to market, she let slip a few choice words to the policeman on the way home. Arrested for being drunk and disorderly, her shame was observed by a reporter from an 1870 edition of the popular magazine *Porcupine*:

*There is a drunken prostitute in the cell already, and into it also she must now go. While one officer stands aside with her child in his arms, she is motioned to a door by the other. One glance in the whitewashed passage is sufficient; in the terror of the moment she attempts a faint resistance, catches the doorway – the brink of despair to her – with both hands and implores them not to lock her up. But this useless spirit of desperation dies out in a moment; and when a strong blue arm goes round her waist, and she is lifted off her feet and beyond the door, she makes no further resistance, and goes off moaning for the child who is now crying as loud as she.*

*One of the officers now sets off to carry the child to the workhouse. It will be there properly tended until three or four o'clock in the morning, when, being again brought to the bridewell it will be restored to its sobered mother.*

Let's listen in to the earlier charging of the other prisoner, the drunken doxy mentioned above, who was now stewing in the cell:

With both hands the policeman grips by the arm a young woman. She is slenderly built and bears no mark of struggling. Without bonnet and shawl, she seems absolutely neat and clean for the locality... When the officer's hard grasp is loosed and she stands at the bar, her eyes, full of tears as they are, gleam defiantly round upon every one and particularly upon the officer who has captured her, while her expression and her whole mien betoken a most superb contempt for the police and the bridewell and everything connected with it. 'Drunk and disorderly in the streets' is the charge made against her.

– Where do you live?

– Oh I live anywhere replies she with a toss of the head which seems to imply that there is little need to ask that. Then turning to her captor:

– You know I am living at Jinny _____'s house now. She tells sullenly where this is and is then asked:

– What are you?

– You know what I am.

The officer speaks the one word she hesitates over and is not contradicted.

– How old are you?

– 21

When the searching begins the ruined girl brings from the pocket of her tawdry, flashy dress, her money. It is tied up in the corner of her handkerchief. She attempts to untie it but cannot see how for crying. The policeman offers to undo it but refusing to let him assist her at last she accomplishes it. She reveals two pennies and a halfpenny. This is all, although it was so carefully stored and nothing more is found upon her.

Then the side-door opens and to the careless, drunken cries that come floating out thence she adds a bitter scream as the officer grasps her again and leads her to the cells. In a moment he re-appears without her.

It's likely that both women appeared in Liverpool police court, whose atmosphere of hopelessness and resignation has changed little over the years. One has the impression that a fellow hack, reluctantly reporting some fifteen years later, is unlikely to be swopping addresses with his courtroom companion:

My neighbour on the right was a woman in the very last stage of dirty raggedness and dishevelment, her hair matted with filth sticking out here and there in stray locks from the bandages with which her head was covered. She appears to have very little on her beyond a ragged gown as dirty as herself, which had evidently never been made for her. Probably it had been brought for a few pence in 'Paddy's Market' or some similar emporium of discarded rubbish.

Little had changed in the same court with the dawning of the new century. Women seemed to be judged by their coiffure and most in attendance were having bad hair days. Let's join a reporter in 1908:

The women hide with a shawl their uncombed hair and hurriedly pinned-on rags of dress. But they leave enough of their face showing to tell the saddening stories of their lives – and also to suggest the sort of lives they lead their husbands. The men wear that slouching contented look which says that any reference to work will be regarded as a personal affront and make them quarrelsome...

The doors of the court are opened and in hurries a little crowd that had been waiting in the street. They jostle one another into the narrow space allowed the public and then they settle down.

The washed, the well-to-do are given seats in front. The contrast makes the picture all the more exciting. One after another in quick succession, eight men and women pass in and out to the space before the dock. They are all very poor. Judging by their clothes, they had little enough money to spend on food, let alone on drink.

It is a quick business. One could fancy that there is a fixed scale of fees.

Most small time offenders were hit in the pocket. An average fine for drunken offences would be about ten shillings, but this still represented a week's money for many offenders who had no choice but to serve seven days at Her Majesty's pleasure in lieu of payment.

Common police-courts were remarkable for the high ratio of women present to view proceedings. Be the accused male or female, the prisoner's mother, sisters, aunts, cousins and female friends would often squeeze into the stalls, all the while mouthing threats and insults under their breath at the policemen and judiciary determined to fine or imprison their loved ones.

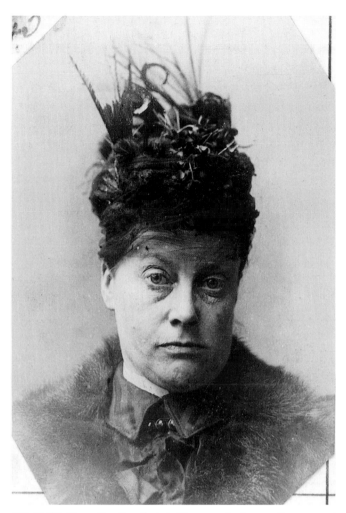

57. Edith Towell, alias Leigh Brown. A domestic servant charged with stealing clothes in Liverpool in 1889 and cash from Rochdale co-op. Three months.

58. Caroline Renshaw. Five years for larceny in Salford, 1880.

59. Catherine Chapman could have compiled a good gaol guide having been arrested in Birmingham, Warwick, Liverpool, Manchester, Accrington and Preston.

60. Helen Lee appears more like a member of the Salvation Army than a thief. 15 months for fraud in Manchester, 1882.

## PERFECT PESTS

Both police witnesses and magistrates were regularly threatened by those they sent for a short break. Sentenced for stealing a ham in Salford in 1874, Ann Davies told the magistrate: *I will make it a dear two months for you.* She was ordered to pay two sureties of £5 to keep the peace once released.

Annie O'Brien was still pleading 'not guilty' even though she had 120 previous convictions for being drunk and disorderly. The 42-year-old was found shouting and throwing bottles in College Street, Rochdale in 1908. This was her tenth appearance here, but she was well known to both the Manchester and Preston constabularies, having notched up over fifty convictions in both places. Sentencing her to one month, the magistrate added *I think that will be best for you, as well as for us.* Annie protested her innocence and was defiant to the last. *I am going down innocent, but I will make the policeman sit up when I come out.*

*61. Women turned their hand to all manner of crime but most thefts were opportunistic and often undertaken under the influence.*

An inappropriately named, Margaret Drinkwater (who drunk anything but), alias Lockett, was charged in Salford with being drunk and using abusive language. The prostitute was further accused of assaulting the two police constables needed to drag her to the station. P.C. Finn had his thumb badly bitten and P.C. McEvoy suffered a torn cheek after Margaret managed to insert her sharp fingernails inside his mouth. The accused had previously served three and six months for assaults on the police:

SIR JOHN MANTELL: (to the prisoner) *I will send you back for another six months.*
PRISONER: (to the policemen) *All right you b_____s I'll do it for you.*

Recalling the prisoner Sir John told her that she seemed a most hardened character and ordered her to be sent for trial at the sessions, where her sentence was doubled.

The Salford magistrates were determined to have the last word. Sir John was once again sitting when Ann Duckett from the workhouse was brought up. She had been 'living' there for three weeks but bluntly refused to do any work in the washroom:

SIR JOHN: *Would you go back to the Union and work or go to gaol?*
PRISONER: *If they want me to go into the workhouse I would rather go to gaol. I have not been brought up to washing.*

Sentencing Ann to fourteen days, Sir John said he would send a letter to Captain Leggett, the governor, asking that the prisoner be sent to work in the washhouse so she would be used to it when she came out.

Another regular workhouse refusnik was the young powerfully built Elizabeth Clarke who did the rounds of the workhouses in the Manchester area in the 1870s. She had no intention whatsoever of doing any work but demanded food and lodging in the tramp wards. With her blatant challenge to authority setting a bad example to other inmates, Elizabeth was locked away in a secure room in Salford workhouse. Here she screamed for hours on end and, when threatened with the police, flew into an uncontrollable frenzy.

Appearing before the magistrates for refusing to work, Elizabeth simply groaned throughout the trial. Following a detailed examination by four medical officers, however, she was deemed to be sane. Elizabeth was ordered back to the workhouse. Once again she refused to lift a finger and was soon back in court again. Kept overnight in a cell, Elizabeth methodically tore all her clothes to shreds. The young police officer charged with bringing her to court explained the bare facts of the situation to his superiors and was ordered to wrap his charge in a blanket. Thus attired she listened as the evidence against her was outlined.

62. *A case of double entry bookkeeping. Although in this case the name is the same, it was not uncommon to find mug shots of offenders who looked identical but had different names listed. Sentences were much heavier for persistent offenders. Mary stole some £80 from her employers, a small fortune for the times. 6 months.*

Elizabeth took her food but when asked to work went into a fit. She had behaved in a similar way in both Prestwick and Manchester workhouses and was a 'perfect pest'. There seemed to be no effective pest control. The magistrates wanted her to return to the workhouse but the guardian was adamant she would never cross his path again. He blatantly refused to let her return. The conclusion of the story is neatly related in the local paper:

*The woman was accordingly liberated, and in the presence of a number of persons who had assembled in the neighbourhood of the court, left the building with the blanket wrapped around her body. She walked down St Stephen Street and proceeded in the direction of Bury New Road, Manchester.*

# OLD BIDDY

The perpetually bowsered Bridget liked nothing more than entertaining a hastily assembled pavement audience with a song, a jig or a little homespun philosophy. Even if they didn't appreciate the performances, whose delivery was often slurred, the crowds in Oldham and Stalybridge knew there would be no lack of incident when 'Biddy' was in town giving one of her al fresco shows. Eventually a policeman would arrive and the second act, 'Biddy's escape' would begin.

Following three days earnest elbow bending and evading the authorities, Biddy's latest jig was rudely interrupted when an officer of the law approached the gathering. She slid off into a house in Waterloo and, with the door safely locked, the self-styled crowd-pleaser lifted the curtains and began to poke obscene faces through the window at the police constable. Pretending to leave the scene, the policeman hid around the corner and Biddy emerged once again to please her audience with her street 'entertainment'. The crowd were there for act two and watched the inevitable arrest, grinning from ear to ear:

63. Ellen Doherty. 14 days for obtaining charitable contributions by fraud.

P.C.: *Now, Biddy, how are you?*

BIDDY: *Ah! Sure! If you'll let me go this toime, I won't make any more bother.*

P.C.: *No Biddy, your promises are no good, you will go with me.*

Biddy never came quietly, instead, as if in an amorous embrace, she swiftly wrapped her legs around the unsuspecting constable and the pair tumbled to the ground. There was no love lost between Biddy and bobby however, as, desperately trying to escape, she swore, spat and struck the arresting officer, who had to call upon the assistance of a man in the crowd. The short trip to the police station must have seemed an eternity as, jeered and jostled by a street mob numbering up to a hundred, the two men dragged, dropped and drew the drunkard along. She was rewarded with a month's stretch inside.

Every policeman had his own particular tale to tell about her antics. Biddy's years drinking had led to her cultivating an impressive beer belly which she was determined to exploit to the full. On one occasion, shortly after arrest, she told the policeman on duty:

*I am very ill, and have a lot of pain in my belly, and think I am going to have a baby.*

The Chief Constable was taking no chances and secretly probably couldn't wait to see the back of her:

*Let her out at once, we do not want any baby born here.*

Both the Stalybridge and Oldham police wanted the dipso off their patches and, rather than arrest her for minor offences, would sometimes pay for her to be transported home, i.e. off their manor.

Although a double handful for the police, Biddy was all politeness and charm before the magistrates. At the sound of the magic words *Bridget Corrigan, stand up* she would stand demurely at the dock rail and flash the odd secret smile at members of the judiciary.

One New Year's Day she grinned and wished the magistrates a happy new year.

The Chief Constable told the court that Bridget had returned to Stalybridge Docks after a stormy voyage on the seas of Oldham where she had notched up roughly thirty-seven convictions. Back at Stalybridge she had a total of about one hundred.

The chairman of the court was far more blunt than would be the case today and obviously wanted the lass to return to Lancashire:

CHAIRMAN: *I wish you would stay in Oldham, we do not want you here.*

BIDDY: *I wish you would let me go, as it is Christmas, and I will go straight out of the town.*

CHAIRMAN: *Oh! No! We cannot do that, you will go to prison for a month.*

Old Biddy began the new year as she had finished the old.

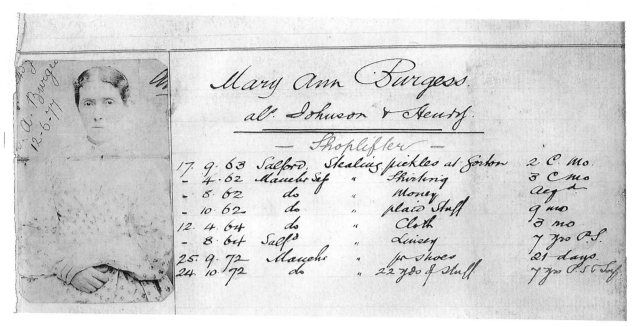

64. Mary Ann started her criminal career stealing pickles and shirking. She has no profession listed save that of shoplifter.

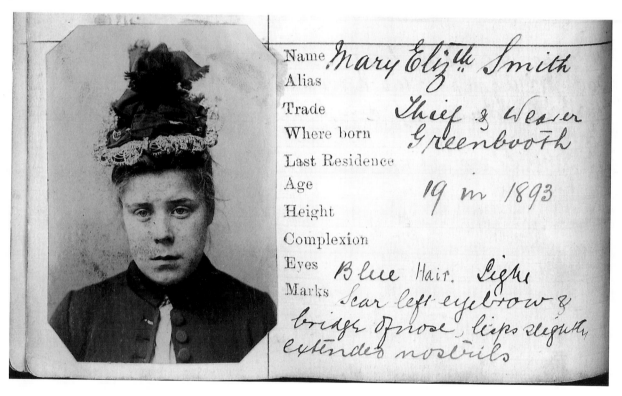

65. Not the best occupation to note down on a C.V.

## THE MOUTH OF RAMSBOTTOM

Mrs Catherine Marsden, the mouth of Ramsbottom, was another regular before the beak. With convictions dating back to 1879, many for brawling, Catherine would give a fat lip to her physical opponents and a lot of lip to everyone else. Catherine was such a regular at Bury Police Court for the use of obscene language that the local paper reported her appearance in 1890 under the headline *A Curse to the Place. A Curse to the Police* may have been more appropriate.

P.C. Tipping told the court that at midnight he found Mrs Marsden giving her husband a tongue-lashing in prime industrial language in Factory Street. The couple were both the worse for wear but the drink brought out Mrs Marsden's frustrations and she berated her poor benighted husband in *very filthy* language. Despite several warnings she just continued ranting and raving. When the Marsdens rowed everyone knew their business.

Mr Heys, the magistrate, who lived on Ramsbottom Lane, close to the Marsdens lodging house in Return Street, had probably had his peace disturbed on several occasions by the mighty mouth. He wanted her out of his court, out of his neighbourhood and out of his life:

MR HEYS: *I tell you what, Mrs Marsden, I wish you and your husband would go out of Ramsbottom for really you are a curse to the place. I would give something towards your going.*

MRS MARSDEN: *Well, I wish I had the money, I'd go.*

Fined 5 shillings, everyone in court readied themselves for the vile torrent of abuse that invariably followed. With expletives deleted the lodging house keeper asked the court:

MRS MARSDEN: *What are you going to do with me next? I have 14 days to come on.*
THE CLERK: *Have you any money?*
MRS MARSDEN: *No.*
THE CLERK: *Then make out a commitment.*
MRS MARSDEN: (flinging down half a sovereign) *Well here's 10s to our Jim's fine.*

Determined to have the last word before returning to Return Street, the mouth threatened that if any police constable touched her on the way out she would shove her fist into him and '_____' quick.

In a case that might appeal to Monty Python fans, Mrs Marsden was again mentioned in court reports, though at least on this occasion she was not in the dock. the whole matter concerned the theft of the Marden's pet canary.

One weekend both their lodger, Richard Fraine, and their canary did a flit. Upon discovery of the crime, the police were immediately summoned, though this time by the Marsdens themselves, not their neighbours. James Marsden, who was a chimney sweep, valued the bird at a rather optimistic £2.

Doubtless aware of this, the offending lodger, having first secreted the bird in a brown paper bag, took it to a 'naturalist', where he sold it for the princely sum of one shilling.

When arrested in the Roebuck Inn, Bury, Fraine claimed that he had taken the canary as compensation for an attack upon his person. He insisted that Catherine Marsden had blackened both his eyes so much so that he could not work. Unimpressed, the beak sentenced him to one

month's bird with hard labour. The bird was returned unharmed to his doting parents. Thirty days in the cage for the thief was as nothing when compared with the canary's life sentence in Return Street condemned to listen to Mrs Marsden until he fell off his perch.

For every old Biddy and mouthy Marsden coming before the courts there were an equal number of young offenders starting their apprenticeships in her majesty's hotels. Despite the popular belief that girls used to do what they were told in 'the old days' many were obviously beyond their parent's control.

Towards the end of the nineteenth century four such young ladies walked the streets of Oldham looking for lads and larks. In July, 1887 Merando Mills, Mary Ann Foley, Margaret E Baxter and Minnie Dearden were hauled before the magistrates. Described in the report as 'young girls' they were arrested, together with some young men, at 1am by P.C. Winterbottom at the junction of York and Manchester Streets. All the youngsters were charged with indecent behaviour. The policeman must have had an air of authority about him as he arrested them all and single-handedly escorted them to the station. His captives were swearing all the while, not as to their innocence but at him – a case of interrupted coitus, perhaps?

Merando Mills was the first to be seen to. Protesting to the court that the P.C. had abused them, the poor lass went down for seven days.

The Chief Constable told the court that Mary Ann Foley had appeared before the bench a few weeks previously after smashing the windows of her mother's home. She had been liberated on the understanding that she would go and live with her sister in Manchester. A policeman had accompanied her there but she was back in Oldham within five hours and had been sleeping on the streets ever since. Mary Ann was given a prison bed for a fortnight.

Margaret E Baxter had been in service but left before Christmas. She told the court that for the past seven months she had been living on money sent by an aunt. Her income had probably come via a sugar daddy or two and, she too, was sent down for fourteen days.

The fourth member of the gang of 'M&Ms', Minnie Dearden was also known to the Chief Constable who had tried to get her into a home. Minnie's mother said that she could 'do no good' with her daughter and would not open the door to her when she came home late. Because her mother adamantly refused to take her back into the family

*66. Ann Oakes stealing clothes from a shop in Rochdale, 14 days.*

*67. 36-year-old Margaret Gregory alias Ann Butler. A life of crime whose last noted conviction was for stealing from the person in Bolton in 1880.*

home, Minnie was ordered to the workhouse pending the making of other arrangements.

It was against the law to birch girls but they might be handed over to their fathers with the court's recommendation of a good whipping. In Salford, 1882 13-year-old Mary Elizabeth Linney received just such a punishment for breaking and entering. Her younger brother, Edward, 11, was given six strokes of the birch by the authorities. There is no record of how many Mary got at home.

There was no real consistency in sentencing. In the same court a young lady Maria Moors, not much older than the Linneys, was sent down for six weeks for stealing a herring worth 1d. The sentence was harsher than normal as the poor girl had previous. Having obvious ambitions of a fish and chip supper, she had been prosecuted the week before for purloining potatoes.

How long would it be before the young apprentices became old pros like Alice Marlor? She

*68. Food surprisingly was not top of the shoplifter's list. Charges of stealing clothes were far more common.*

had one surefire way of avoiding court appearances though. When her name was called in the Oldham court in 1887 the Chief Constable told the magistrates: *In this case the woman refuses to dress herself. She is in the cells and she says she is poorly.* Remanded on charges of importuning for the purpose of prostitution, Alice was seen by a doctor. With clothes and charges dropped, Alice was removed to the workhouse to knit, pick oakum and no doubt swop stories with her Oldham neighbour, young Minnie Dearden.

## BOTHER IN BLACKBURN

Tens of thousands of minor offenders appeared before the courts in Victorian Lancashire. Many did not come quietly. Typical of such cases were those featuring in the July 1880 editions of the *Blackburn Times*. They included:

*Mary McLoughlin was charged with being drunk and disorderly in Water-street – on the way to the station she was very rough – fined 10s. and costs.*

*Jamie Gallagher and Catherine Gallagher, man and wife, were summoned for being drunk and disorderly in Bolton-road on Sunday evening. The male defendant did not appear. They were both fined ten shillings and costs upon which the female exclaimed that the first time she came across the "bobby" she would thump him well. She was again placed in the dock and charged with using threatening language and the fine was increased to twenty shillings with costs or one month in gaol.*

In the same court Mary Margerison, *a powerfully-built woman* appeared in the dock with a baby in her arms. This practice was fairly common, though whether to elicit sympathy or whether there was nobody else to look after the tot, varied from prisoner to prisoner. Mary was charged with committing an act of gross indecency in a passage off Warwick-street one Saturday evening, another example of *coitus interruptus*. The man did a runner but Mary was fined five shillings.

Shops were frequently criticised by the police for tempting potential shoplifters by openly displaying their wares. Elizabeth Kenyon, a 34-year-old weaver, just had to have the boots on display

*69. In the days before police started taking their own photos of offenders they would take a copy of portraits, if available, to add to their files. Elizabeth King was sent down for five years in Manchester though her offence was not noted.*

outside the pawnshop in Addison Street. Regrettably she did not have the necessary 2s. 6d. to buy the boots so was forced to help herself, secreting the footwear beneath her shawl. Sentenced to a brief spell inside, Elizabeth, obviously a novice at the game, collapsed and had to be carried to her place of incarceration.

There was no such drama with the experienced. In Blackburn, 1882, the appropriately named 53-year-old Ellen Pickup was charged, together with her daughter Nancy Smith, 24, with stealing shawls. Mum was discharged, but naughty Nancy got three months.

Under the headline *A Hungry Female* the Blackburn court reporter told the tale of Ann Johnson, who made off with 2lbs of mutton, value 1s. 8d., whilst her local butcher was in the backyard. In anticipation of a nourishing stew later that day, Ann adjourned to her local in Church Street for a few aperitifs. Picked up paralytic a few hours later, the missing mutton was found secreted about her person, tied up in her handkerchief. A meal of bread and gruel was her menu for the next two weeks.

Inside Ann would have had to keep a sharp eye open for Margaret Robinson. She had a reputation for doing serious damage to strangers for no apparent reason. One woman she took offence to, Elizabeth Leeming, was first verbally and then physically assaulted by Margaret in the Rosebud Inn, Grimshaw Park. Seized by the hair, Elizabeth was struck violently in the face, had both eyes blackened and her nose rearranged. Intimidation is no new problem. When told that she was being summoned Margaret did not mince her words:

*Tell her if she sends me to gaol she can get her b_____coffin ready.*

Fined 40 shillings with costs or one month, it's highly unlikely the Blackburn brawler had the readies and went away for a sojourn in her second home.

Nothing was safe from light-fingered domestics who often obtained employment using forged references and departed into the night weighed down with their employers valuables. Isabella Lee Hargreaves, 31, from Laurel street, Blackburn was brought before the court for stealing her

70. *Elizabeth Ogden, Elizabeth Robinson and friend in Brewery Street, Salford. The police criticised the layout of shops as they were a temptation to shoplifters.*

mistresses' drawers (Is nothing sacred?) valued at 1s 6d. She was sentenced to 14 days with hard labour.

## LIVER BIRDS

Liverpool lasses were no more law-abiding than their Blackburn sisters. Indeed, with most crime being committed under the influence, a spot of bother was far more likely to occur in Liverpool than anywhere else, as the following figures demonstrate. They show the number of male and female drunkards arrested, per thousand of population:

| | |
|---|---|
| LANCASHIRE | 6.3 |
| LIVERPOOL | 31.25 |
| WIGAN | 14.75 |
| BOLTON | 11.3 |
| MANCHESTER | 10.5 |
| LONDON | 5.0 |
| ENGLAND/WALES | 4.75 |

Charlotte McMahon was charged with being drunk and disorderly, assaulting the police and doing wilful damage. At ten past four on a Saturday afternoon in 1884 the carousing Charlotte ignored the advice of P.C.17 to go on home (well, maybe these weren't his exact words) following a disturbance on Derby Road. In response Charlotte cuffed the officer around the head, broke his whistle and tore his coat. It took three policemen to drag the hysterical hyena to the station, where she promptly broke a drinking can upon four plates of glass in the cell. It appears that the most serious offence was the tearing of the coat (14 days): the assault on the policeman warranted just 7 days and a fine of 1s 6d was imposed for damaging the windows.

Having been before the courts on some forty drink-related charges, Mary Cohen, described in the 1880 *Liverpool Journal* as *a young woman of rather masculine appearance*, determined to give up drinking for good. Unfortunately, a few minutes after making this life-changing resolution, Mary faced her first challenge – her father was arrested.

Seeing him being led to the police station Mary immediately waded in, kicking and punching. Arrested for the forty-first time, all Mary could hope was the judge would take pity on her: *Your worship, I was after coming from the League Hall where I signed the pledge.* The next three months Mary spent in a state of sobriety that probably far exceeded the judge's, serving hard labour at Her Majesty's pleasure.

Sharing accommodation was an economic necessity but few, if given any choice, would have chosen to live with Ann Glennan of Bostock Street. She appeared in court just one week after Charlotte McMahon. Described as *a woman of dissipated appearance* she stood in the dock cradling a baby in her arms. Ann was prone to flip with no warning and would destroy everything in the house she shared with several fellow lodgers. One Monday afternoon, after smashing a jug of beer, her cohabitants coerced her into a small room and locked the door. Over the next two hours she hurled abuse and insults at her gaolers, all the while beating against the wooden panels. A policeman called to the scene told the court that she threatened to 'break through and trample on them like frogs'. Charlotte was ordered to pay 2s. 6d. damages and 5s. costs.

## PARALYTIC IN PRESTON

For two viragos appearances in the courtroom and the odd spell inside were a mere inconvenience to their chosen way of life – being permanently paralytic in Preston. In October 1880, Mary Ann Rigby and Ann Cotterall were charged with being drunk and assaulting Ann Bridges and Jane Derwent. They were further arraigned for assaulting P.C.s Jackson and Duxbury and breaking two glasses – value 8d. – in the Duke of York on Darwen Street.

Both the accused, along with a male accomplice, were provided with beer in the vaults but, considering them to be already drunk, the barmaid refused to serve refills. With the glasses now obviously being of no further use, both Mary and Ann took careful aim and launched them across the room in the direction of Jane, the barmaid who had called time upon them. A fellow imbiber joined the affray but was badly cut on the hand when defying the drunken duo. Upon arrest the outraged offenders desperately endeavoured to break their shackles and violently assaulted and spat upon the

71. *Some things old, nothing new, some things 'borrowed' some things blue.*

arresting constables as they were hauled to the station.

In Court and probably in their usual state, the girls treated the whole matter as a joke, repeatedly bursting into fits of laughter whilst evidence was being given. They were given one month compulsory sobriety time.

## TWO SAVAGES

Esther Savage and Esther Savage Junior, mother and daughter, featured in the top ten of Bootle's police court black list. Senior had completed a century of convictions, whilst her young prodigy was a mere 77 not out. Both women were appropriately named and were destined to spend most of their lives locked away. Reporting on Junior's 78th conviction in 1897 the court reporter shows just how rowdy the courtrooms became when taken over by the Savages:

[She] *launched into a terrific volley of execrations and curses which comprehensively embraced the magistrates, the witness and Police Constable Fox who received her at the bridewell. Her language was of an atrocious character, and during the whole of the hearing of her case she never ceased the filthy stream of objurgations which outraged the ears of all in court.*

Sentenced to three months, Savage Junior vented her spleen at the nearest official, cutting the lip of the officer who occupied the dock with her. She was dragged away biting and scratching two police officers, *fighting like a wild cat.*

The Chief Constable asked the magistrates to immediately parade her in the dock again for the assaults upon the police but, visibly shaken, they were only too pleased to see the back of her and refused the request.

Another aptly named soak was Elizabeth Urine who was found, well let's say... drunk and disorderly in Salford.

In the same newspaper that revealed the antics of the two Savages the journalist was feeling a little mischievous. Sent to report back on a temperance meeting he wrote:

*Mrs Bent said she had been in the district 58 years and had been 22 years an abstainer. Ever since she had been an abstainer it had been 'sunshine' with her'. This remark was followed by a sharp shower of hail which threatened to put a stop to the proceedings.*

## 'COME AND BE SHAVED'

Described as *a well-known inebriate* there was little hope of any sunshine in the life of Susan Wilson. She would attend Salvation Army gatherings, not to bash the tambourine but to beat any officer in uniform. Hauled up before the Salford courts on a charge of being drunk and disorderly and assaulting Joseph Ashton, a member of the Salvation Army, Susan put up a spirited defence. With sixty-four previous convictions she appeared at ease in the familiar surroundings of the courtroom. The case against her was outlined in the summer of 1882. As the Army marched along William Street, Susan was said to have punched Ashton on the side of his head. The churchman managed to hold onto her until a policeman arrived.

Perhaps predictably, Susan had a different version of events:

PRISONER: *I simply asked the man whether he could tell me the catechism before he began to preach and he began to laugh at me. (Laughter). He then said to me 'come and be shaved'. He could not say 'saved'. I said to him 'I have got a few coppers in my pocket and I won't rob the barber'. Then a woman from the Salvation Army said 'Will you please buy a book?' I said 'No. I'll have a gill'. (More laughter). Is not that so?*

COMPLAINANT: *No*

PRISONER: *See he will not tell the truth here although he preaches the gospel to the people.*

MR MAKINSON (magistrate): *I'm sorry I can't send her away for 12 months in order to keep her off drink.*

PRISONER: *Oh by _____ don't do that.*

MR MAKINSON: *One month with hard labour.*

PRISONER: *No. I won't have a month, I will have two.*

This said, Susan fought tooth and nail with those trying to take her down. With every other word unfit for publication, she was wrestled down swearing revenge on both the police and court officials. Her defiant words still echoed throughout the courtroom long after she was out of sight, physically manhandled to her customary cell.

## TIRED OF LIFE AND FOND OF GAOL

Court reporters grew to know their subjects well and would introduce them with familiarity. In Oldham 1887 *the well-known* Mrs Austerberry, a landlady, made one of her regular appearances for being drunk and irresponsible. Dreading the prospect of being locked up, she would always pay the fine. The publican appeared to be on good terms with all present and accepted her punishment with good grace. When told that she would have to pay five shillings the recidivist replied: *Is that your price this morning? I will pay it.*

The same reporter appeared to enjoy the appearances of another local dipso. Under the headline *Winifred O'Brian Once More* he wrote that Winnie appeared *with one of her best smiles on her face.* The journalist knew Winifred's pattern of behaviour reporting that she *indulged in her usual amusement viz breaking a cell window.*

Gaol held no fear for Elizabeth McGinty, indeed, having been convicted thirty-six times it was hardly her second home, it was her first. Under the headline *Tired of Life and Fond of Gaol* the middle-aged gaolbird's case was reported from Dale Street police court in April, 1880. The charges were all too familiar, being drunk and riotous and assaulting P.C.s 930 and 905 and an old man. The evidence having been heard, Mr Raffles remarked that the prisoner seemed to treat the matter as a good joke and asked her what she had to say for herself:

PRISONER: *I only came out of gaol yesterday, so it is as well for you to keep me altogether. It would be a great favour to me if you would send me to the sessions and get me 12 months – that is what you can do with me, because I am tired of my life.*

MR RAFFLES: *It is a great expense to the country to keep such people. You are a great nuisance; you must go to gaol for three months, with hard labour.*

PRISONER: *Sure, that's nothing, why did you not send me to the sessions at once?*

Elizabeth would almost certainly have come across Ann Craze in her tour of prisons and police cells. Ann did not have to be asked to be strip searched, she voluntarily began divesting herself of her clothes on every occasion she was arrested, and there were many. Charged with drunkenness and disorderly conduct at the house of a relieving officer, Ann (clothed on this occasion) pleaded her case.

PRISONER: *When I asked him for relief he struck me and told me to go back to prison where I came from.*

RELIEVING OFFICER: *I never was near you.*

PRISONER: *You pushed me out. You are always upbraiding me.*

There was no real choice between a ten shilling fine or a two week stint in stir, Craze didn't possess ten pence.

Those who could, reluctantly paid their fines but there were occasions when disputes as to who was to blame for offences spilled out of the courts. There was no shortage of recriminations in the cold, sober light of day once the best part of a week's money had been handed over in fines. In 1899 a reporter from the *Social Gazette* was all eyes and ears as penniless prisoners left court:

*...The fateful door opens and out comes a woman and two men whose very countenance betray them. She has evidently been fined, and considering – as is generally the case – that the iron degree is unjust, blames her companions in a voice resembling a series of piercing shrieks, which increase in volume as she nears the main*

*outlet. It is getting exciting; the men retaliate in unchivalrous language, the loafers seem to be temporarily electrified and rush out to witness the issue.*

Despite appearances, however, if any funds remained, the dispute was probably settled a few minutes later, around the corner in the local pub.

Why, one may wonder, did so few cases of attempting to bribe the police appear before the courts? One such accusation stands out because it was so rare. Emma Thompson from Salford, whose profession was listed as prostitute/thief made a proposition to an arresting police officer: *If you try and square him* (a man she had relieved of 9s) *I'll give you half-a-crown.* She should have known better than to attempt to influence one of the boys in blue and was sent down for four months.

Two and six, I ask you!

## ATTACKED WITH A KNIFE AND FORK

Although Bible teachings would have us love our neighbours, it is still not easy today, let alone in the overcrowded Salford slums of the 1870s. Mary Butler was charged with violently assaulting her next door neighbour, Ann Cavany. Mary lost her rag one day accusing Ann of sitting on her doorstop in an alluring manner trying to entice her (Mary's) husband. For this alleged provocative pose, Ann was rewarded with a blow to the nose with a basin. Whether she wanted her fire poking or not was unclear, but Ann seemed to be half-expecting the attack and retaliated with three stabs of the poker to her infuriated rival. Mary was sent down for three months with hard labour. Would Mr Butler be calling on Ann for a cup of sugar in Mary's absence?

Although most domestic disputes saw the husband in the dock, this was not always the case. Resourceful wives defended themselves with whatever came to hand. Once again in Salford, in 1874, Mary Riley was sentenced to six months for striking her husband on the head with the *chamber vessel*. Displaying no remorse whatsoever she told the arresting officer that she would give her husband three times as much when she came out.

In Liverpool Sarah Cordonay was tired of her common law husband's persistent whining. On August 12, 1863 the beleaguered man complained that his steak had no gravy. Sarah playfully admonished him by pricking his nose with her fork. Ten minutes later, following a serious scrap, she finished him off with her knife. Sarah was sent down for four months for manslaughter.

72. *For some appearances in the dock were shaming, others positively enjoyed themselves and would roundly insult judges, police and witnesses.*

A typical case played out in Salford Police Court was reported in the Christmas 1882 edition of the *City Lantern and Free Lance*. The reporter appears to be full of the Christmas spirit and his description captures the atmosphere of the police courts of the time:

*'Mary Malone, come forward.'*

*Mary Malone, who has hitherto been concealed from view, in the back part of the wire-topped cage behind the dock ascends the two steps leading to the standing place, guarded by two policemen, folds her arms across her apron, smiles and tries to look the picture of injured innocence, but fails. Mary is a big strong woman, with red hair, and arms that would make a pugilist feel uncomfortable. In her sober moments she is a washerwoman, but occasionally is so overcome by her feelings and beer that she forgets herself, breaks her neighbours' windows for amusement and threatens those who object.*

*Just now, Mrs Malone looks as if she had been sleeping in the gutter all night. Her apology for a dress is covered in mud, and her hands appear as if they have been recently engaged in clearing a stopped-up drain pipe. Two policemen with black eyes, bruised faces and torn uniforms, testify to the fact that Mary was a little excited on Saturday night. They found her breaking windows, uttering bad language, and making*

*it lively for everybody objecting to her mode of keeping Christmas. When they endeavoured to persuade her to come to the police station, she struck the officers with a poker, hit them with her fists, kicked them with her feet, and finally had to be brought to head quarters by six policemen on a stretcher.*

MAGISTRATE: *I'm afraid you're a bad woman Mrs Malone.*

MRS MALONE: *Is it me? I wouldn't hurt a fly your honour. I'm a respectable widow woman without a chick or a child to care for me. Tis a lone woman I am this blessed minute.*

*The prisoner caught up a corner of her apron to catch the coming shower.*

MAGISTRATE: *Don't cry here madam. It won't do a bit of good; besides we have had enough wet this season.*

MRS MALONE: *Shure, can't I shed a tear?*

MAGISTRATE: *Not here, Mary. Keep back the cataract until you go below, and the man in the charge-office will give you a brand new tin coffee can so that you won't flood the cell.*

MRS MALONE: *Tis joking you are.*

MAGISTRATE: *We never joke here, Mary. Life is too short for jokes. Call the next witness.*

73. Salford Flat Iron Market - the place to go for cabbage and pig's cheek.

Mrs Flaherty, a little woman, ornamented with a discoloured optic, a cut lip, a mob cap, a shawl and a strong brogue now took the stand.

MRS FLAHERTY: *Please your honor, this is the greatest blaggard that ever stepped in shoe leather.*

MRS MALONE: *Don't believe a word she says, your worship, she's the biggest liar between here ____.*

MRS FLAHERTY: *No I'm not, sur. I'm a respectable married woman... On Saturday night I went to buy some cabbage and a pig's cheek for the Sunday dinner. I went down to the Flat Iron Market.*

MAGISTRATE: *But we have nothing to do with the Flat Iron Market...*

MRS FLAHERTY: *And as I was saying, your worship, says I to myself, if I can get anything cheap, shure it's at the Flat Iron I will get it says I.*

MAGISTRATE: *Mrs Flaherty do you know you're wasting the time of the court; and that all the people are getting thirsty. Just leave the Flat Iron behind you and turn back to your own street.*

MRS FLAHERTY: *But I haven't got there yet, sur.*

MAGISTRATE: *Then I'm afraid, Mrs Flaherty, you'll have to defer the description of your visit, though the market price of pig's cheek might be interesting to some in the gallery. What did the prisoner do to you?*

MRS FLAHERTY: *Look at me face, yer honor, and see what the blaggard has done to me.*

MRS MALONE: *Oh! if I could only get hold of you Mrs Flaherty.*

The prisoner made an attempt to get over the dock front but was dragged back by the officers standing on each side of her, amid an outburst of expressive language.

MAGISTRATE: *Call the next witness.*

Michael Moriarty made his way into the box vacated with a flourish of conscious dignity by Mrs Flaherty. Mr Moriarty seemed as if he had been struck by a battering ram; patches of plaster covering nearly the entire portion of his features.

MR MORIARTY: *Just look at me face yer honor. Isn't it a nice sight I am, sur, and it's all through that dirty blaggard, Mary Malone.*

MRS MALONE: *He's the greatest ould liar that_____.*

His worship gave Mary a twelve months' hard labour look that made her break off in the middle of her sentence.

MR MORIARTY: *Well, sur, the new tay pot, that I gave fippence for, hadn't been standing on the hob above five minutes when a stone came flyin' through the kitchen window and knocked it into the fire and broke it. I went to the door, when who should I see but Mrs Malone trying to prise up a paving stone with a poker, to throw through my windy… She struck me on the head and face until I was covered with blood.*

MAGISTRATE: *Have you anything to ask the witness Mrs Malone?*

MRS MALONE: *Do you think I'd demane myself to ask a question of a man who only earns sixteen shillings a week on the railway?*

DETECTIVE SUPERINTENDENT: *There's no more witnesses, sir.*

MAGISTRATE: *I am sorry for you, Mary. This is the tenth time you have been here Mrs Malone, and though I pity your emotional feelings, I shall be obliged to prevent you getting excited again in a hurry.*

MRS MALONE: *Only give me another chance, yer worship, and it's me that'll be the decent woman. I'll never touch _____.*

MAGISTRATE: *Mrs Malone, you have made the same promise nine times and ten times you have attacked your neighbours with pokers, and broken their windows with paving stones. You have worn out a first-class stretcher in being bought to the station, and black eyes have been at a premium among the police in your street whenever you have given way to your feelings… You can now step back Mrs Malone, and I'll make arrangements for finding accommodation in prison for you for six months and a front seat in the van.*

MRS MALONE: *Six months! Mother of Moses; it is six months you'd be after giving me. Oh! you hoary headed vagabond! Do you think I"m going up for six months. Norra a bit will I stir.*

*Mrs Malone grabbed the dock front as if she meant to take it with her to celebrate Christmas Day by a bonfire in her cell.*

*A policeman caught hold of each arm. There was a wrench, and a bundle of police. Mrs Malone and bad language shot suddenly back into a heap at the bottom of the two steps, followed by a scream and a whoop that would not have disgraced a Sioux Indian on the warpath. Then a door was heard to open, Mary's yells became more subdued, and finally died away as she was carried into the cells below.*

NEIGHBOURS IN CONFLICT

*74. Mrs Malone would smash the windows of those not paying her laundry bills.*

Some crimes were far more cold and calculating. In the Liverpool of 1880, 40-year-old Margaret McCann set about her neighbour, Margaret Neiles, with a hatchet in her home in Hyslop Street. As the victim lay prostrate and gushing blood from a wound to her forehead, McCann's husband rushed forward clenching a mallet to finish the job. The axewoman deemed her enemy had received her dues and held him back: *Don't do anything to her, I have given her enough.* Rushed to hospital with a fractured skull, Margaret Neiles could not be pronounced out of danger until the wound healed. Having already served six sentences for assault, Margaret McCann could expect no mercy, nor was she shown any being ordered to serve twelve years penal servitude.

The sanity and mental health of women like Mary Butler and Margaret McCann must come into question. Under the headline *'A Batch of Liverpool Savages'* a report appeared in 1874 whose contents, if published today, would surely elicit more sympathy than ridicule. Indeed, today nearly all the offenders would be considered ill rather than evil. Just one case from the list is representative. Catherine Eccles, a woman with a violent temper, was charged with having dangerously assaulted Jane Dignem. One Saturday evening she poked some cayenne pepper and cotton wool under Jane's front door and promptly set it alight. A stifling obnoxious smell passed through the dingy rooms and, when Jane emerged coughing and spluttering to confront her neighbour, she was kicked to the ground and two of her ribs were broken.

## CONVERSION ON THE ROAD TO OLDHAM

As the heavens opened even salvationists must have been losing faith that Sunday in 1912. The Manchester weather outside the Angel Hotel in Oldham Road was living up to its reputation. Thoroughly drenched, they also braced themselves for the habitual onslaught of projectiles and vile, verbal abuse that went with the territory.

The Salvation Army could not be accused of choosing easy targets. They deliberately marched, sang hymns and preached in the most dangerous and deprived areas of the city. The Angel Hotel was the local of the infamous scuttlers, whose gang members were renowned for secreting razors in the peaks of their caps. The biggest challenge to the Army, however, came not from the disadvantaged, drunken and desperate young men – but from a 49-year-old woman, whose detestation of the police and salvationists was legendary. As Nancy Dickybird, soaked in both senses, prepared to vent her own self-loathing on God's volunteers, what some may see as a modern day miracle was about to take place before the eyes of both believers and boozers alike.

To understand the enormity and importance of the event a little of the history of Nancy Dickybird needs to be revealed. Born Nancy Gradwell in 1863 our heroine would, from a young age, deliver her fathers's meals to his place of work. With his being often being employed as a steeplejack, Nancy became nimble and very strong on her sandwich rounds and was the only girl ever to climb the greasy pole at the Old Blackley fair. A happy girl, she would whistle while she worked and was given her affectionate nickname by her doting father. Her early years were typical of the times, illness followed by grinding mill labour and injuries sustained at her work place. Nancy married a labourer, Joseph, and bore two children. Stories later circulated that he was a wife-beater and drunkard, unfortunately only too typical of many men at that time. Whether Joseph drove her to drink or whether she was heading down this well-worn path is unknown, but for whatever reason Nancy took to the bottle like a baby to the breast.

Nancy, with the zest of a convert, quickly degenerated into one of the thousands of drunken sots infesting the stinking streets of slumland Manchester. Every penny was spent on booze, with the result that her children were taken into care. Not only was Nancy a drunkard, she was the worst form of that species, an aggressive, obnoxious woman who would trade insults and punches with anyone and everyone, both male and female. And she certainly held her own. Being an extremely strong and powerful woman, many police constables would give her a wide berth when finding her laid out on the pavement the worse for wear.

Anthony Burgess, of *Clockwork Orange* fame, remembers stories about Nancy as told by his stepmother, who was the landlady of the Golden Eagle in Miles Platting:

75. The cause of Nancy's downfall. Ironically this drawing featured in the Salvation Army newspaper.

*There was a fearsome character known as Nancy Dickybird, whose violent approach was signalled by runners – 'Nancy's coming'. The main bar would clear on her entrance, and my stepmother would greet her with a truncheon and knuckledusters. There was an extensive armoury available for defence, including two army revolvers complete with ammunition. Nancy would sail into an ecstasy of foulness, urinate on the floor and then leave.*

Throughout her drinking days, Nancy Dickybird served an astonishing 173 terms of imprisonment, nearly all alcohol-related. Being unable to pay any fines, Strangeways became her second home. Forced to sober up inside, Nancy cleaned and scrubbed the prison floors and became a very proficient laundress. Unfortunately, she could not clean-up her own act and was often arrested in her usual state of inebriation just hours or days after release.

*76. In a most remarkable conversion, Nancy Dickybird went from hitting the bottle and odd policeman to hitting the tambourine.*

There appeared no hope of redemption. Few drunken gaol-birds approaching fifty-years-of-age ever changed their ways. The Army's raison d'etre, however, was salvation and they were about to be rewarded with a prize recruit.

As a drunken woman stood gently swaying in the wind, a Salvo called Mrs Walsh stepped forward and offered her the shelter of her umbrella. This small unexpected act of kindness from a perceived enemy was to change Nancy's life for ever. She suddenly fell to her knees. Joined by Captain Walsh and his wife, the trio knelt on the pavement and engaged in fervent prayer to the Almighty. Nobody noticed the elements though all those present had an inner glow.

This tale of singing in the rain must surely have inspired Anthony Burgess.

The hardest woman in Manchester, the scourge of police and publicans alike was on her knees, with her 'enemies' about to change her life forever. The Lord did indeed work in mysterious ways. Nancy was taken to the Walsh's home where she was fed and clothed at their expense. She was also found work as a magistrate's cleaner. A relieved police force rewarding her with a gift of bedding.

Publicans, now a little out of pocket but with a great deal more peace of mind, subscribed to her first uniform. The Salvation Army found Nancy a house at 28, Annis Street, Harpurhey and she was soon re-united with her children.

For the rest of her life she devoted herself to the cause that had saved her. Nancy became one of the Army's most famous speakers, touring the country telling the story of her past life and conversion. She later returned to her old drinking haunts – to sell the *War Cry*. Nancy took to her religious work with the same enthusiasm she had once taken to the bottle and spent the best part of her later life doing God's work. She died in Crumpsall Hospital in 1931 and her funeral at Harpurhey Cemetery was attended by one of the largest crowds ever witnessed in Manchester for such a ceremony.

Nancy's favourite hymn will come as no surprise:

*I was wandering in the wilderness*
*Far away, far away,*
*Jesus sought me in tenderness,*
*Happy Day, Happy Day*

# THIEVING, LYING, DISOBEDIENCE, RUDENESS AND IMPROPRIETY

Throughout the late nineteenth and early twentieth centuries Mount Vernon Green and Toxteth Park Girl's Reformatory were home to about two thousand antisocial Liverpool adolescents. Reformatories were finishing schools for the criminal classes, who felt they owed nothing to the society that had incarcerated them. Contemporary reports highlighted the inclinations of the institutionalised girls to *thieving, lying, disobedience, rudeness and impropriety*.

Details of some of the girls' crimes show just what a cunning and devious clientele peopled the 'prison'. In July 1885, the children of Toxteth were terrorised by a teenager named Catherine Fay. She would stop young girls running errands for their parents and purloin pennies from their tiny fists. 4-year-old Elizabeth Kellett was Catherine's fifteenth, and for the moment, final victim.

The terrified little mite was on the way to the pawnbrokers clutching 3s 9d close to her chest when she was stopped by the big girl. Elizabeth was warned that a deaf and dumb man was waiting to attack her around the next corner. He was going to steal her money and chop her fingers off! Catherine offered to 'hide' the coins by wrapping them in paper so that the young girl would not be attacked. The terrified Elizabeth agreed and her 3s 9d was replaced with a wrapped parcel containing just 4d. Catherine then ran off. Remanded for a week for enquiries, she was sentenced to ten days followed by a lengthy stay in the reformatory.

Another young woman who preyed on vulnerable children was Margaret Everett who began her criminal career as an 11-year-old and served more than seven years in institutions of various kinds before her twentieth birthday. Having graduated, she became quite an accomplished thief. In the Spring of 1880 a spate of child-stripping and robbery cases alarmed mothers in Bootle, Seaforth, Waterloo, Walton, Everton, Kirkdale, Wavetree and Fairfield. Many children were relieved of errand money and, in every case, robbed of their boots. The predator's *modus operandi* was to persuade youngsters to walk with her by promising them toys and clothes.

Margaret changed her dress regularly and never committed her crimes in the same neighbourhood on consecutive days. She was apprehended by chance when an ex-constable noticed her talking to a child outside Christ Church school in Bootle

77. Ellen Williams was a very cunning and devious young offender. She would go to inspect furnished rooms pretending to be a respectable music teacher. After inspecting a room in Stretford Road she told the landlord: 'This will be the place for me as there will be no man to be met with. The instant a man comes into the room where I am I turn my back upon him.' The 'music teacher' would make off with anything she could carry once securing the key to the door. She had 16 convictions in Manchester and 3 in Salford.

and followed the couple, via a series of back entries, to a field at the back of Walton prison, where the inevitable robbery took place. He then trailed Margaret to her place of employment, Mr Hartley's Jam Works, and subsequently reported the events to his former colleagues.

Many teenage girls were simply running wild. 14-year-old Ann Macarthy was sentenced to 21 days imprisonment followed by five years reformatory for *skinning* – stealing clothes from young children and pawning them. Her mother told the court that she was wild and untruthful and beyond her control.

Margaret and Ann would almost certainly have

made the acquaintance of 15-year-old Ann Griffiths, whose speciality was 'ringing the changes'. Ann went to a hotel in Walton road and asked for some whiskey in a small bottle. Having been supplied with the liquor, she demanded change from the two shillings she said she had handed over. In fact the amount was far less or she had not paid at all. Losing her bottle, the respectably-dressed girl took flight but was apprehended and handed over to the police, who knew her well. Superintendent Walsh told the court that she had been living a *fast life* for the previous two years.

Another difficult daughter, who spent a few weeks in the Liverpool reformatory in the 1870s was Elizabeth Ann Marsden. On returning to her Salford home she *resumed the bad companionships which seem to have been the cause of all the trouble.* Discussing her case with a Mr Birley, the chairman of the school board, her parents determined on a course of hard love. The decision was made to send the 15-year-old Elizabeth to the other side of the world. In this case *the first loss would be the best loss* according to her parents.

The **S.S. Durham** left Plymouth for Adelaide on February 24th 1879. Along with several girls from Swinton Industrial school, Elizabeth's new address was to be the services home in the capital of South Australia. Adelaide was not to her liking and she quickly moved on to Melbourne, which proved no more appealing. What went through her parents' minds when they read her last letter home? It was written by a friend and dictated by Elizabeth:

*I wish I never left home. I am very miserable and always regret the day I came out here. I am in the hospital I was in before and went out, and I had to come back again with rheumatic fever. When I go out I hope to get a situation and make some money to go home never to leave you. Melbourne is a bad place, full of bad people and I am very unhappy...*

Elizabeth finished with some lines from a half-remembered poem:

*My child, I can no longer hide thee*
*So to my God alone confide thee*
*Thus spoke a mother broken-hearted*
*As from a darling child she parted*
*Though far from you I thus have strayed*
*Still in thine arms I fly afraid*
*And to my mother's gentle breast I fly*
*O guide me through the storm.*

78. *No space was wasted in the delinquent girls home at Ford, near Liverpool. There was barely an inch between the beds.*

79. *The girls were forced to work long hours in the laundry by the cleanliness-is-next-to-Godliness brigade of nuns.*

The letter listed an address but all subsequent communications to it were returned marked 'Unknown'. And so, too, is the fate of Elizabeth Ann Marsden. Did she become a Sheila and adapt to her new home country? Did she die destitute in a land she detested? Did her parents really make the best choice for both her and them? Research by her great-niece Norma, living in Bolton, has traced her to Sydney in 1889, but from here the trail goes cold.

## REFORMATORY LIFE

Meanwhile back in Blighty only about one in ten reformatory inmates could read and write to a *satisfactory standard*. Older girls worked in the laundry whilst their younger counterparts were trained in needlework, cooking, household work and knitting.

Living in such proximity both the girls and staff were vulnerable to epidemics such as diphtheria, scarlet fever, typhus, smallpox, tuberculosis, measles and chicken-pox. Youngsters infected with smallpox were ordered to isolation hospitals and girls suffering from consumption, especially those having no family or friends, were sent to the workhouse to die. Although not fatal, cases of ringworm, eczema, impetigo and diarrhoea appear all too frequently in the doctor's records.

Given the raw material they had to deal with, reformatory staff neither expected nor indeed received a transformation from foul-mouthed hardened hussies to demure and obedient maidservants. A report from 1880 reveals some of the problems they faced:

*The inmates seem to be drawn from a still lower stratum than ever before and are very unpromising materials. To raise such a class from the depths of depravity and utter neglect in which they have been sunk, is indeed a work of Christian charity and mercy; but it is one of labour and difficulty, and only a certain amount of success can be anticipated.*

Nonetheless, if official figures are to be believed, a high majority eventually went into service or to live with friends. What the figures do not show is how long they stayed in employment or just how many went on to spend long periods in prison.

The girls drove some of their teachers to drink. A Miss Riley returned after one necessary session at the pub with *hat askew, her eyes glazed and smelling strongly of gin*. The sewing mistress's demand for a supply of beer for medicinal purposes was dismissed out of hand. A Miss Parkinson was forced to resign after boxing one of her charge's ears.

In the early years of reformatories girls' punishment took the form of strokes of the birch, hair cropping and a diet of bread and water. Dormitories were locked at night and the girls were forbidden to speak at mealtime. With the relaxation of these rules in the early twentieth century, staff found discipline difficult to enforce and among the girls rates of violent conduct, refusal to work and theft increased. With filthy language now being directly targeted at them, several staff took lengthy absences *broken down in health*.

At Toxteth Park Girls' Reformatory, 9 Parkhill Road, probably the toughest institution in Lancashire, Miss Struthers, a young, attractive and enthusiastic matron, lasted little more than 24 hours. Having arrived on the evening of March 18th, 1912 she was, by the following afternoon, faced with a full-scale riot. In the only report she ever made to the authorities, Miss Struthers gave her account of the troubles:

*I entered on my duties here on the evening of the 18th. Next day at 1.30pm 18 girls refused to pay any attention to the bell summoning them to work, and remained in the yard dancing and singing. After the Assistant went for them they came to the workroom and then 10 only started to work, the remaining 8 refused to obey any orders. They disturbed the house and neighbourhood by dancing, singing and marching around the room, jumping on the forms and continued to do so for four hours. At 6 o'clock, Mr Jones arrived and they were asked to apologise. All did but one girl named May who refused absolutely and a constable was called in. While she was being allowed time to consider, some fighting ensued among the girls who had apologised, and a hysterical girl outside the workroom broke a window. For twenty minutes the scene was one of a riot; Finally May was taken to Essex Street Bridewell.*

After probably the shortest spell in charge of any institution, the hapless Miss Struthers resigned and was compensated with an award of £7.10s.

80. Anything up to 120 girls were in residence at any one time.

*81. It was hoped that girls would learn the skills to enable them to get a job in service.*

*82. Sewing and knitting formed a major part of the curriculum.*

# HELL IS THE WOMEN'S WING AT WALTON

Several of the Toxteth girls probably went on to higher education in Walton.

If ever one could imagine a hell on earth it would surely resemble the women's wing at Walton Gaol, Liverpool. Here all manner of misfit, dropout, dipso and mentally unstable inmates would goad each other into fights, sing and scream for hours on end, and generally stick two fingers up at anyone who crossed their paths. That warder who had maybe eaten too many pies, or was perhaps follicly challenged, needed to be as thick-skinned as most of his charges were thick-headed. Verbal assaults were merciless.

In 1869, some 6,819 sentences were served by women in Liverpool. Many were released and back inside a few days later. Despite the best efforts of the warders the silent regime could not be enforced. In 1871, *The Liverpool Mercury*, reporting that the adult females appeared more wicked than the males, continued:

*The drunkenness and depravity of certain classes of the female population of Liverpool appear to be something considerably beyond what it is to be witnessed elsewhere. Most of the offenders are in prison for drunkenness. Many have been in prison a considerable number of times, girls of twenty have been committed six, seven and eight times each and even girls under sixteen are in gaol for drunkenness. Men appear more frightened of solitary confinement than women. Women also fear less 'short commons' – short rations.*

Basil Thomson was appointed as Deputy-Governor to the prison in 1896 and would try to avoid the female cells at all costs. He described their occupants as:

*…rougher than any primitive women I had met in the South Seas or elsewhere in odd corners of the earth.*

In *The Criminal*, his book of reminiscences, he continued:

*I have said that the female prison was worse than the male. It used to be my duty to see off the discharges at seven every morning. The routine was to go to the female prison first. The entry of the Governor or Deputy-Governor was the signal for the thirty or forty women who were assembled in their own clothes for discharge to begin to sing, not the same tune, but any tune that they could think of, and the songs were interspersed with loud personal remarks about their visitor's appearance.*

*When it came to calling over the names, the noise grew deafening, because at that moment every woman was determined to be heard above her fellows. Mr Walker, who was not generally tolerant towards indiscipline, made no attempt to check the noise. He said it only made them worse, and if you punished any of them the news would go round Liverpool and you would be set upon in the streets. I said I would like to try. He replied. "Then try and see."*

*Next morning, when I could make my voice heard, I announced that until the noise stopped no one would be discharged. There was, in fact, power to retain any prisoner until midnight on the day of his discharge. The announcement behaved like a hand grenade. For a moment one might have heard a pin drop and then – I was glad to get out of the room.*

*The women used to march from the female prison to the main gate singing at the top of their voices, probably to attract the attention of the men who were also assembled for discharge. To the men I went, and the contrast was extraordinary. If a man whispered to his fellow there was a sharp "Silence, there!" from the warder, and there was not another whisper.*

The female prisoners in Liverpool were amongst the most hardened cases in the land. Many would use fouler language and demonstrate far greater disregard for the prison authorities than their male counterparts. A rookie chairman of the Prison Commission was given a tour of Liverpool Gaol by Basil Thomson, who noted:

*I remember taking a wicked delight in showing him the Liverpool women as a sample of the material for which he had to legislate. I thought that I detected a faint blanching of his cheek as he emerged from the female wing.*

Liverpool ran a creche in the prison for mothers with very young children and those who ended their confinement in confinement. The general rule was that no baby over twelve months old was permitted to stay in gaol, but where there was no suitable alternative, and when the mother's sentence was over a year, the rules were occasionally bent a little.

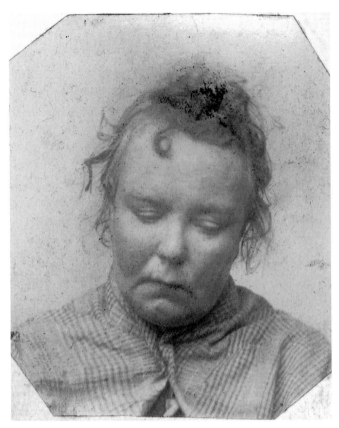

83. Mary Higgins spent several years in Walton on charges of stealing money, clothing, a watch and chain and for being a rogue and vagabond and reputed thief.

Basil Thomson recalls the effect the presence of a baby had on many of the female internees:

*A baby disorganizes the entire female prison, from the matron downwards. Everyone wants to play with it, and, as sunshine is followed by storm, so the baby causes jealousy and uncharitableness to divide the oldest friends. The landing cleaners who work outside their cells used to compete with one another for the privilege of holding the baby for a moment, and the only person who never seemed to get a "look in" was the mother.*

Starved of affection, the girls and women took to anyone who showed a little interest in their plight and the matron became one of the most loved and admired women within the walls. She had the power to restore a little sanity within the insane demimonde. When inmates smashed windows or tore up their clothes she would plead with, comfort and pacify them. Offenders would invariably stop their destructive action and burst into tears in the arms of one of the few people who showed them anything resembling understanding and compassion. The matron would affectionately call the inmates her 'gurls'. Only once did the Deputy-Governor witness his star worker become upset:

*A "gurl" had come into prison with golden hair, and this, proving to be a wig, was plunged into a bucket of disinfectant, from which it emerged not golden, but green, with all the curl taken out of it, which meant of course a claim for damages, and a wig might cost anything. But there was worse to come. She rushed into my office, shaking with emotion, and said, "Sir, you remember the 'gurl' with the golden wig that turned green; well, sir, she's not a 'gurl' at all, but a man.*

The overspill from Liverpool took their defiant attitude to Lancaster:

*A man would be put upon bread and water again and again for minor offences, or for not doing his work satisfactorily; but he rarely kicked up a row, or refused point blank to do his allotted task. But with the women it was different. The monotony of prison life was more irksome to them; so on the slightest pretext they would break out – perhaps smash the windows and tear up their clothing.*

*A male officer was generally sent for to lock them up in the 'refractory cell' which meant no bed and bread and water for three days and three nights. But to secure them in the first instance sometimes required no little strategy, for they would arm themselves with a formidable weapon in the shape of a rubbing-stone placed in the foot of a stocking, which they would swing round with more or less violence, the nearer you approached them or kept at bay.*

84. Francis Cross aka Edith Shaw specialised in stealing portmanteaus from railway stations in Manchester and Liverpool.

# TO BE HANGED BY THE NECK

## THIRTY LASSES SENTENCED TO DEATH

COL 1: DATE OF TRIAL

COL 2: NAME OF MURDERESS

COL 3: LOCATION OF TRIAL

COL 4: WAS MURDERESS RELATED TO VICTIM?

COL 5: OUTCOME AFTER APPEAL

WOMEN SENTENCED TO DEATH IN LANCASHIRE 1860-1914

| | | | | | |
|---|---|---|---|---|---|
| 1. AUG 1863 | ELIZABETH BENYON | LANCASTER | YES | *P.S. LIFE |
| 2. DEC 1866 | NANCY ARMFIELD | LANCASTER | ? | P.S. LIFE |
| 3. MAR 1869 | SARAH CRAWFORD | LANCASTER | YES | P.S. LIFE |
| 4. DEC 1870 | CHARLOTTE ELLIOTT | LIVERPOOL | YES | 10 YRS. |
| 5. DEC 1872 | CATHERINE HANLON | LANCASTER | NO | P.S.LIFE |
| 6. MAR 1873 | MARY DAVIDSON | LANCASTER | YES | P.S.LIFE |
| **7. AUG 1874** | **MARY WILLIAMS** | **LANCASTER** | **NO** | **HANGED** |
| 8. JULY 1877 | MARY BENNETT | MANCHESTER | YES | P.S. LIFE |
| 9. JULY 1877 | SOPHIA TODD | LIVERPOOL | NO | P.S. LIFE |
| 10. NOV 1877 | ANN CARTLEDGE | MANCHESTER | NO | P.S. LIFE |
| 11. JULY 1878 | ELLEN LANIGAN | LANCASTER | YES | P.S. LIFE |
| 12. MAY 1879 | EMILY JONES | LIVERPOOL | YES | P.S. LIFE |
| 13. FEB 1880 | MARY ANN TRACEY | LIVERPOOL | YES | P.S. LIFE |
| 14. NOV 1883 | ELIZABETH SCOTT | LANCASTER | YES | P.S. LIFE |
| **15. FEB 1884** | **CATHERINE FLANAGAN** | **LANCASTER** | **YES** | **HANGED** |
| **16. FEB 1884** | **MARGARET HIGGINS** | **LANCASTER** | **YES** | **HANGED** |
| 17. FEB 1884 | SARAH MALLINSON | LANCASTER | NO | P.S. LIFE |
| 18. JUL 1885 | ELIZABETH LANE | LANCASTER | YES | P.S. LIFE |
| 19. NOV 1885 | MARGARET HIGGINS | MANCHESTER | YES | P.S.LIFE |
| **20. JUL 1886** | **MARY BRITLAND** | **MANCHESTER** | **YES** | **HANGED** |
| **21. FEB 1887** | **ELIZABETH BERRY** | **LANCASTER** | **YES** | **HANGED** |
| 22. AUG 1889 | FLORENCE MAYBRICK | LIVERPOOL | YES | 15 YEARS |
| 23. NOV 1889 | JANE JONES | LANCASTER | YES | P.S. LIFE |
| 24. MAR 1890 | ELIZABETH MAPP | MANCHESTER | YES | 5 YRS. |
| 25. MAR 1897 | CATHERINE KEMPSHALL | LIVERPOOL | NO | P.S.LIFE |
| 26. APR 1898 | ISABELLA COOKSON | MANCHESTER | YES | P.S.LIFE |
| 27. DEC 1902 | EVA EASTWOOD | LIVERPOOL | NO | P.S.LIFE |
| 28. DEC 1902 | ETHEL ROLLINSON | LIVERPOOL | NO | P.S.LIFE |
| 29. JAN 1904 | MARY ANN BOYLE | LANCASTER | YES | 1 YR. |
| 30. JUL 1910 | MARY ELLEN MOORE | LIVERPOOL | YES | 4 YRS |

*P.S. = PENAL SERVITUDE

*The cursed rimes of the secret poisoner*
*We must confess are the worst of all*
*You bless the hand that smooths your pillow,*
*But by that hand you surely fall.*
*You put your trust in those about you,*
*When you lie sick upon your bed,*
*While you are blessing they are wishing*
*The very next moment would find you dead.*

Although penned about Durham's serial poisoner, Mary Ann Cotton, the broadsheet ballad could equally apply to her numerous Lancastrian sisters in crime. Most murderesses were convicted of doing away with members of their own families. Husbands and children were poisoned for being 'in the way', a financial and social burden – or for financial gain stemming from insurance payouts.

Until 1851 arsenic was one of the most favoured means of dispatch. Cheap, colourless, odourless, soluble in hot water and more or less tasteless, arsenic produces symptoms not unlike those for diarrhoea or cholera. Many a hard pressed doctor could have mistakenly listed these common illnesses as the cause of death.

After 1851, however, buyers of arsenic were required to provide names, addresses and reasons for their purchase but, as it was in general use, this was not a great inconvenience. Those requiring a secret stockpile could simply soak flypapers. The main problem for Victorian poisoners was that burial rather than cremation was the favoured form of funeral. Arsenic traces remain in corpses for years and if, at a later date, foul play was suspected, exhumation was a simple procedure.

When women murdered members of their families they did not always operate as cold-blooded poisoners, means and motives abounded. Low paid workers, who lived in, frequently farmed their babies out. Maids and nurses would visit their children on the odd afternoons they had free but often, could barely afford the minder's fees. Most scrimped and saved to meet their obligations but a small minority took the agonising decision to kill their own children for economic reasons.

## YOU ALWAYS HURT THE ONE YOU LOVE

Most of the thirty females sentenced to death were extremely callous and showed little remorse for their victims only a small number were genuinely contrite.

17-year-old **Elizabeth Benyon** (No.1) from Eccles threw her twelve-month-old child in the river with a large stone tied around its neck. The unmarried mother first told police that she had given her child to a woman from the Swan Inn, who had recently lost her own baby. When this was disproved she promised to tell the truth if the police did not lock her up. Elizabeth subsequently confessed that she had met a man in Deansgate who suggested the means of disposal. The defence argued to no avail that the child was already dead when thrown into the river.

**Nancy Armfield** (No.2) the one that got away. Despite hours of research no reports of her crime could be found.

In Great Lever, just three days after Christmas 1868, **Sarah Crawford** (No.3) was told by her landlady, who had eight children of her own, that there was no room in the inn for either herself or her 20-month-old child. Weaver and child set off into the wet and windy night. Sarah returned without her charge saying she had found lodgings for the baby. With the discovery of a body, she gave herself up with the words *I did drown it in the lodge; it's no use denying it.*

**Charlotte Elliott** (No.4) was a southern girl who came to Liverpool in an advanced stage of pregnancy to take ship to the U.S.A. She wanted to start a new life alone in the land of opportunity and slit her baby's throat seconds after its birth. The defence argued that she had used the murder weapon, a knife found in the room, to help with the delivery but nobody believed the story. Charlotte remained in a silent world of her own throughout the trial but collapsed as the death sentence was announced.

**Catherine Hanlon** (No.5) was a hawker living just above the breadline. When she saw a boy stealing one of her apples she seized him by the collar and instinctively stabbed him in the abdomen. He died from an inflammation of the bowels.

In November, 1872, **Mary Davidson** (No.6) a domestic servant, picked up her young daughter, Carrie, from her carer's in Manchester and set off on 'a little holiday'. Leaving the train at Lancaster the pair were spotted by an observant nine-year-old girl who was attracted by Mary's distinctive black muff with white spots. Mary was seen leading

85. A vast majority of the victims of murderesses were members of their own family.

the little girl down a footpath in the direction of Aldcliffe and observed two hours later returning without the child. Mary boarded a train to Carlisle. A search of the area made by two police sergeants led to a pond where the lifeless remains of a female child were discovered.

Meanwhile the mother had returned to her workplace in Northenden and told the baby's minder that she had left her daughter with relations in Carlisle. Mary Davidson's remarkable muff was to prove her undoing. Everybody seemed to notice it and, following interviews with rail passengers in the North West, she was traced to her place of employment.

In defence Mary stated she had murdered her daughter because her new sweetheart did not know that she was a mother and she feared he would leave her if he found out she came with 'baggage'. The case caught the attention of the public and several thousands had to be turned away from the courtroom. Mary was reprieved on the very eve of execution.

For every Mary captured and condemned there must surely have been many more mothers whose children conveniently disappeared to 'relations in the country' never to be seen again. It was just a case of Rover being sent to the country.

## MARY, MARY QUITE CONTRARY

*Mary Williams had shot a poor labouring man,*
*At Bootle near Liverpool, deny it who can;*
*She said t'was her husband the weapon had fired*
*But better proof of guilt could not be desired*
*She has left seven children her fate to bewail*
*To remember their mother was hung in the gaol*
*But guilt does not hang on their dear little heads*
*They'll sleep the sleep of the innocent as they lie on their beds.*

*Mary Williams was heard ere the drop was let fall*
*To utter the prayer 'May God bless you all'*
*Bless and protect my children so dear*
*They'll scorn their poor mother I've reason to fear.*

It was very rare for women to use firearms in their murders. **Mary Williams** (No.7) was hanged in 1874 for just such a crime. The verses composed and sold following executions served as a cruel obituary.

Life in Victorian Lancashire was harsh and brutish for most women but poor Mary Williams' thirty years on the planet must have been a veritable hell on earth. Born in poverty, her mother died when she was just two. A drunken father who paid her scant attention ran off to the States with another woman ten years later. Mary, abandoned in Bootle without any education, became a street walker.

Some years later she married a man who, over a drunken decade, simply used her for his sexual needs. Somehow seven children from the union managed to survive the destitution and drunkenness. As a temporary escape Mary herself took to the bottle. In the Summer of 1874 she was one of the main protagonists in a massive women's brawl in Raleigh Street, Bootle, that was said to have continued on and off for a period of hours.

What happened following the bloody brawl was contested by Mary to her dying day. What the prosecution alleged was that Nicholas Manning, the brother of one of the women Mary had been scrapping with, was shot as he walked past her house. Mary was said to have produced a pistol from under her apron and fired at the 27-year-old, who had played no part in the dispute. Nicholas died from blood poisoning some two weeks later.

The victim was heard to cry: *I am done for.* To which Mary was said to have replied: *Yes and there are two or three more I will do it to before the night is over.* Mary later told an arresting officer: *It was me who shot him and it is an honour to my country.*

As in childhood so in maturity, Mary was again abandoned. Whilst awaiting trial Mary's husband disappeared, abandoning the children, the youngest of whom was only three-months-old, to the workhouse, and leaving his wife to face the rope alone. Indeed, so friendless was poor Mary, that at the start of the trial nobody had been employed to defend her. An emergency attorney was appointed at the last minute with very little time to acquaint himself with the facts. He told the court that the reason for her husband's disappearance was because it was he who, standing behind Mary, had fired the fatal shot.

Mary wept bitterly as the judge donned the black cap.

Although probably of no consolation whatsoever to her, Mary was not hanged alone, being executed along with Henry Flannagan on 31st August 1874. Like many of her predecessors in a similar position, Mary found God at the last and her last words were spoken with the fervour of the convert. Mary repeated the Lord's Prayer, the Hail Mary and the Apostle's Creed.

To the very end Mary Williams blamed her absent husband for the shooting. Mounting the steps of the scaffold she noticed some reporters and insisted: *Upon my conscience gentlemen. It was my husband fired the pistol.*

Mary Williams was the first woman to hang in Kirkdale for 31 years.

The body of **Mary Bennett's** (No.8) son John was identified by its clothes, which had been issued by Stockport workhouse. The jury were out for just two minutes. Mary's final words to the court were: *I did not do anything with the child except put it in the water.*

## TAKE THE MONEY

Secreting the body of a dead child in a box for over a year does not seem the action of a sane, sensible and intelligent woman. Most people who met the attractive 28-year-old governess **Sophia Todd** (No.9) during her sojourn in Lancashire in the 1870s may well have used all three adjectives. Appearances can be deceptive.

Born in the West Indies, the daughter of a Scottish civil engineer and a local woman, she travelled to England as a child following the premature death of her mother. Sent to be educated in Brussels, Sophia showed an aptitude for foreign languages and became fluent in six. Spending several years in St Petersburg as the governess of a Russian Prince she quickly mastered both Russian and Polish. When her father fell on hard times she returned to England and obtained posts with several noblemen. Later she went on to teach languages in Lancaster. Her marriage to a farmer in Liverpool was not a success as the farm did not pay. Sophia was forced to find employment as a barmaid at the Victoria Hotel. Her husband went on the railways before he, like her mother, died in his twenties.

Times were hard for widows of whatever age. Sophia saw an opportunity to make money in the baby farming business and placed an ad in the

**THE TIMELY WARNING**

86. *Arsenic was the most popular poison. The lives of husbands could be insured without their knowing. Let's hope this potential victim spots the subtle warning.*

*Liverpool Mercury.* Whether she at first intended to coldbloodedly murder her charges or just 'lose' them is unclear. Her first 'adoption' resulted in the baby being found abandoned in the street. The second was 'found suffocated'. Her third advertisement was placed in the *Mercury* on 9th July, 1875.

*Wanted, by a respectable married couple, a child to adopt and bring up as their own – premium required.*

One evening a short time later, in reply to the advertisement, a man arrived at her lodgings in the inappropriately named Prospect Street, Liverpool. Cradled carefully in his arms nestled a boy some 3-4 weeks old. Passing Sophia ten pounds he said he did not wish to see the baby again. That night the governess slit the unnamed infant's throat and secreted the body in a tin box. Sophia changed lodgings several times over the next few months and, like Mary's lamb the box was sure to follow. Eventually the stench became so obnoxious that, following Pandora's example, Sophia's landlady opened the box. She must have wished she'd

taken the money instead. Sophia was promptly arrested; the case finally came to court two years after the murder.

Somewhat desperately Sophia's defence attorney claimed that the baby boy had suddenly died in her arms as she was undressing him; medical evidence showed otherwise. Throughout the hearing at the Liverpool Assizes Sophia wept, but her tears had little effect on either judge or jury. Following the verdict the black cap was donned:

*Sophia Martha Todd, you have been convicted on evidence which has abundantly satisfied the jury that tried you, during a long and patient investigation, of the crime of wilful murder. I cannot but say that I agree in the verdict which the jury themselves have pronounced… on the night in July, when this poor little innocent baby was brought to you, it was brought for its destruction, and ere the morning sun dawned you barbarously murdered it. I desire not to harrow up your feelings by recounting to you the dreadful scene which you must have gone through that night. The law prescribes but one punishment of this crime of murder, and that is the punishment of death.*

Flanked by a turnkey and female warder, Sophia Todd showed no emotion as she walked firmly from the dock. A petition was signed by some two thousand sympathisers who thought the punishment too harsh. One Saturday afternoon, shortly before the scheduled hanging, a telegram was received at the gaol stating that the medical evidence was not conclusive enough to enforce the death sentence which was consequently commuted to life imprisonment. When told the news by the chaplain, Sophia was seized by a fit of hysteria lasting several hours.

**Ann Cartledge** (No.10) was tried for the murder of Elizabeth Coleman in Manchester. It was just one of many abortions that were botched even though Ann was a midwife who should have known better. Elizabeth died of peritonitis and gangrene three days after the 'operation'.

Following her sentence to death **Ellen Lanigan** (No.11) made an impassioned plea for her life: *I wish to tell the truth and plead for mercy; it was poverty and distress and not cruelty that made me drown my children… I have cried about my children every day since.*

When Ellen's husband was confined to an asylum, she was left to try and raise their four young children by herself. Ellen eked out a living selling ginger beer and sweets in a Liverpool shop but was forced to take in a lodger to help with the rent. The lodger, a drunken worthless man, *took advantage of her lonely position* and Ellen fell pregnant again. Whether the fact that she bore twins pushed her over the edge is not recorded. Seven weeks before the birth their father moved out. After having the babies in Liverpool Workhouse, she abandoned one in a clay pit on Stanley Road and the other in an ashpit on Brisbane Street.

20-year-old servant **Emily Jones** (No.12) paid a nurse to look after her 15-month-old daughter. With the father contributing nothing, the childminder's fees so high and her wages so low, Emily could see no alternative but to do away with her baby. She confessed to the police after the body was discovered by her sister in her clothes box: *I took it out on Sunday night and strangled it. I am only a poor servant girl and could not afford to keep it.* Described as *an interesting looking girl* Emily stared at the floor throughout her trial and needed to be carried from the court after sentence of death was passed

*87. Some callous baby-farmers would deliberately throw the baby out with the bath water.*

## PLEADED HER BELLY

Despite not having the benefits of today's technology the police in Victorian times had a reasonable clear-up rate for two reasons: many murderers confessed or committed suicide, and the majority of the guilty who protested their innocence were just plain daft.

A rookie copper in his first week on the job would have seen the glaring inconsistencies in the Widnes murder of 1879. The case was tried in Liverpool. The victim was Patrick Tracey and the accused were his wife, Mary Ann and two lodgers, 30-year-old Hugh Burns and 21-year-old Patrick Kearns. The late Patrick Tracey was considerably older than his 28-year-old wife, who, as a landlady, took the first half of her job description – as provider of bed and board – quite literally.

In September and October 1879, a pregnant **Mary Ann Tracey** (No.13) started shopping around for insurance premiums for her husband. One policy for £100 was taken out with the Prudential and another for £250 negotiated with the Accidental Insurance company.

With a nice little nest-egg to fall back on, a bun in the oven and a strapping 21-year-old labourer to replace her old man Mrs Tracey saw him as entirely expendable. After three conspirators agreed on their story, the worker from Muspratt's chemicals was coldbloodedly dispatched to the next world with a shot to the head.

The story told to the police was that, in the early hours of the morning, a burglar broke in downstairs and stole £15. He then went upstairs, entered the Tracey's bedroom, and shot Patrick as he lay in bed, his wife and child just inches away. The police were immediately suspicious. Firstly, the window where the alleged intruder had made his entry was still dirty and the cobwebs undisturbed. Secondly, there was not one spot of blood on Mrs Tracey's nightdress.

Further investigation uncovered a trail of debt. The Tracey's owed monies to most of the local tradesmen – so how did they come to have £15 secreted downstairs? The murder weapon was found some twenty yards from the house and enquiries quickly determined that it, along with the bullets, had been purchased locally by the thirty-year-old labourer, Burns.

Both lodgers were arrested. In his cell the second boarder, Paddy Kearns, who was probably the father of Mrs Tracey's unborn child, sought to apportion blame on his co-accused. He made a statement relating to his movements from 2am on the day of the killing:

*I was awoke by a call to rise quick. I got out of bed and got my shirt on, and I came to the room door, and Burns was standing at the head of the stairs at Tracey's room door, fully dressed and he had the candle and stick in his hand, and Mrs Tracey was standing at the room in her nightdress and the baby in her arms. She was screaming and shouting. I said what's wrong? She said Oh I am shot and my darling husband's shot. Burns was all of a shiver on the stairs and trembling, and he could not hold the light so I took the candle out of his hand. The room was very dark and smoky and I seen Pat Tracey lying in bed at the far side, and I*

*called him and he made no answer. I looked at him and saw he was murdered. I then went downstairs. Burns said 'Look at the door open and the window raised!' I looked out of the back door, and held out the light, but saw no one; but I heard some footsteps to the back yard, but I could not see anyone.*

Kearns concluded his statement by stating that he saw Burns holding a pistol:

*It was Burns that shot him, and no one else.*

Unable to collect the £250 insurance, because her husband's death was not accidental, Mary Ann Tracey was herself arrested following the Coroner's inquest.

Along with her two co-accused, she listened attentively as the damning evidence against her was revealed in court.

June Burns, a young girl, attested to the tension in the household. One morning shortly before the murder she had been in the Tracey's house nursing the baby. Instructing her not to answer the door if Mr Tracey returned, Mrs Tracey then went upstairs with Paddy (Kearns). When Mr Tracey did return unexpectedly, he was left kicking his heels at the front door for a full ten minutes. Once his wife let him in Tracey immediately stormed upstairs. Confronted by the lodger in his bed, he turned on his wife:

*This is the second time I have ketched you, and Paddy must leave the house.*

On another occasion the young girl had seen the lodger strike Mr Tracey. This caused his wife to burst into raucous laughter, which was only halted by a vicious slap from her husband. All was clearly not well on the home front.

When the jury heard the doctor's evidence about the absence of blood on the nightdress and police testimonies about the cobwebs on the window and the positive identity of Burns as the purchaser of the pistol, they needed just twenty minutes to find all three guilty.

Dr Commins addressed the judge:

*My lord, as the prisoner is quick with child, I ask that the proper legal steps be taken.*

Mrs Tracey was granted a stay of execution.

In Kirkdale gaol several women friends visited the condemned Paddy Kearns who insisted that neither he nor Burns had shot Mr Tracey.

*Well Paddy* they asked *Don't die with a lie in your mouth. Let it be known who did it.*

Paddy replied: *No I shall not; but I shall write a*

long statement tonight and you will know how it was done.

If the statement was written it was never released. In semi-darkness and a blinding snowstorm the two men were hanged at Kirkdale Prison. Two mystery visitors attracted the attention of one of the reporters present:

*Shortly before eight o'clock two disreputable women, gaily dressed, drove up to the gates of the prison in a hansom cab. They conducted themselves in that free and easy manner characteristic of such persons, and one of them, who was attired in a loud bonnet and a sealskin jacket, was so demonstrative as to warrant the suggestion that she had been drinking something stronger than tea for breakfast. When they were*

*assured that the execution was over, they ordered the driver to 'go it' as fast as he could to town; and the ebullient one laughed loudly and winked at the policeman.*

Meanwhile Mary Ann Tracey sat brooding in her cell. Whether she'd known at the outset that she could *plead her stomach* or whether, indeed, she had actually pulled the trigger will never be known. Her sentence was changed to penal servitude for life on appeal.

**Elizabeth Scott** (No.14) put her ten-day-old son in a parcel and sent him from Southport to Stalybridge where he was discovered with a handkerchief over his mouth.

88. The cold-blooded sisters who murdered members of their own family for financial gain.

# THE BORGIAS SISTERS

## Kirkdale gaol, Liverpool. March 3rd. 1884

*All 'squalid' Liverpool was there. The crowd consisted of very young men, boys, girls and women. Hardly one of the latter had a bonnet on and they appeared to have hastily thrown shawls over their heads.*

*At seven o'clock snow began to fall, and a few minutes afterwards the swamp which fronts the gaol was completely covered...*

*The prison bell began to toll at a quarter to eight o'clock and a rush was made to the wall where criminals used to emerge in the days of public execution with the hope of hearing the 'thud' of the drop. It is utterly impossible to hear anything of the kind, but the populace insist that they can detect the sound.*

*At a minute before eight o'clock the procession leading the culprits came through the small door of the main building. It was headed by the chief warder who was immediately followed by Flannagan, who leaned heavily against the Rev. Father Bonte, and a warder, and repeated the 'prayers for the dying'. Binns followed close to Flannagan. She was ghostly pale and her eyes were apparently closed.*

*'Into thy hands, O Lord, I commend my spirit.'*

*'Lord Jesus receive my soul.'*

*'O Lord, be merciful to me a sinner.'*

*'Jesus, son of the living God, have mercy on me.'*

*were the aspirations and prayers that with trembling lips, but inaudibly, the miserable women tried to repeat after the good priest as they clung to the warders for support and slowly and with effort ascended the cruel flight of steps.*

*Flannagan walked with the greater difficulty and was followed more firmly by Higgins. The culprits were*

89. The story of Mrs Flannagans flight as related by the Illustrated Police News.

*immediately placed under the beam...*

God would have had to have been at his most merciful to forgive the callous, cold-blooded crimes of these two members of his Roman Catholic flock. The sisters were found guilty of murdering their nearest and dearest for the most inhumane reason – financial gain. The case was a vulgar tragedy of low life.

Despite being illiterate, **Catherine Flannagan and Margaret Higgins** (Nos 15 and 16) managed to insure the lives of a number of their family members for substantial sums just prior to poisoning them with arsenic obtained from boiled flypapers.

Woe betide anyone who fell ill in the sisters' household in Skirving Street, Liverpool. Once a family member went down with an ailment the doctor was called in and the 'patient's' life insured, without their knowledge, for considerable sums. The sisters, nicknamed the 'Borgias' by the press, then 'nursed' the sufferers by providing them with drinks laced with arsenic.

Two of their first victims were John Flannagan, Catherine's 22-year-old son, and Margaret's stepdaughter Mary Higgins (10). Catherine told a neighbour that her son was very ill with consumption and *would go off like all the rest and never live to comb a grey head.* Mary Higgins and another victim, the daughter of one of Catherine's lovers, were disposed of in the same way.

John Flannagan was buried on 9th December, 1880 with the sisters duly collecting some £23.2s in insurance. As the deaths of young people were far more common in Victorian times, the sisters' ploy of bringing in a doctor once a family member fell ill worked well. The medical men's suspicions were not aroused when the patient died a few days later.

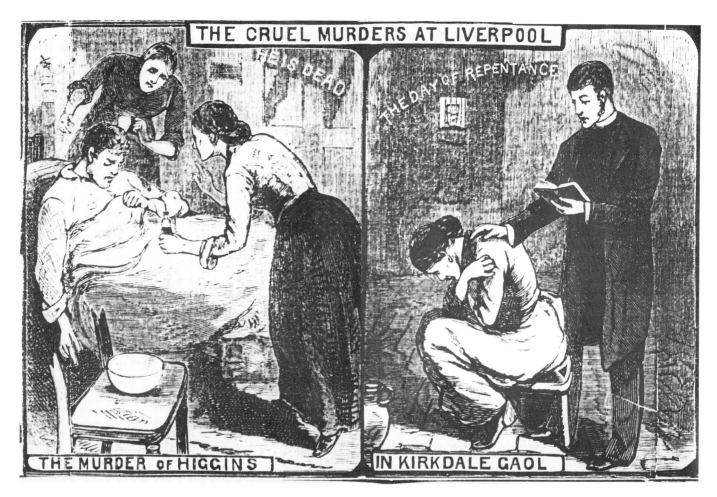

90. *The murders so shocked the public that up to 10,000 tried to gain access to the courtroom. Both women lived on in wax effigy at Madame Tussauds for nearly one hundred years.*

Following these deaths, all seemed to be going according to plan for Flannagan, the 55-year-old lodging house keeper, and Higgins, her 41-year-old charwoman sister. But one evening the women shamelessly took to the bottle and, with their guards down they let slip the truth about the earlier deaths, and a great deal more. A neighbour, Maria Hoare, overheard the sisters quarrelling in the pub about the death of Higgins' first husband, a man named Thompson:

HIGGINS: *You poisoned my husband.*
FLANNAGAN: *He wasn't your husband – he was your fancy man and an old Orangeman.*

When Maria began to spread the story, also accusing the elder sister of murdering her own sons, she was taken to court on a charge of slander and ordered to pay the offended sisters the princely sum of £5. This too went the same way as the insurance money – down the deep throats of the dipso duo.

Meanwhile, despite the court ruling, poisonous rumours persistently circulated about the manner of life and death in the sisters' families.

In 1883 and again short of funds, the crafty, calculating couple selected their next victim – Margaret Higgins' hapless husband, Tom. Out for a big killing the women insured Tom Higgins with four different companies for a total of £91.00. They even tried to obtain a policy worth £50 from the Royal Liver Friendly Society but this required a medical. When the doctor called to examine Tom he was chased away with the words *To hell with you and your club* ringing in his ears. Tom must surely have had an inkling that he was not much longer for this world.

In court a neighbour described his passing:

*Tom had a terrible thirst and asked for a drink. Mrs Flannagan filled a spoon from a bottle, but he refused to drink it. Then I poured him a glass of water and held it to his lips. This time he did drink, saying, 'Oh God bless you' and suddenly his head rolled and he was still. I said 'Oh, Mrs Flannagan he is dead.' I lifted his head onto the pillow and she told me to mind my own business and let him die in peace.*

By this time the ugly rumours about the sisters had reached Tom Higgins' brother, Patrick, who persuaded Tom's physician to request a post-mortem as a result of which, Margaret was remanded in custody. Fearing the worst, Catherine disappeared into the back streets and alleys of Liverpool's slumland. A handbill headed MURDER was issued by the police.

91. Catherine Flannagan was thought to be the sister who administered the poison.

*We wish to know the whereabouts of Catherine Flannagan, suspect in a murder case; and anyone with such information is requested to contact the Central Police Office. Mrs Flannagan is about fifty years of age, 5ft. 2ins in height, stout built, full features, fresh complexion, freckled face, dark eyes, dark wavy hair turning grey; has two teeth out in the front of the upper jaw, scar from a cut mark on the upper lip, thick lips, cut mark on left eyebrow, small nose slightly turned up, wears large gold-earrings and has several rings on her fingers, speaks with a strong Irish accent. Resided at 145, Latimer Street, Liverpool and was last seen on the fourth instant dressed in a black dress, black shawl and bonnet… She will no doubt endeavour to leave the country, having friends in America.*

Mrs Flannagan was apprehended a couple of weeks later. She had never left Liverpool. Once Tom's body was found to contain arsenic the police exhumed the remains of John Flannagan and Mary Higgins. Despite having been in the ground for three years, John's body was in a perfect state of preservation. The intestines were covered by a yellowish sort of deposit suggesting poisoning by arsenic. Mary's body, which had been in Ford cemetery for just over a year, was in a similar state.

On February 15th an enormous crowd, most of whom were female, assembled outside St George's Hall anxious to obtain admission to the trial. The court was filled almost as soon as the doors were opened. Many thousands, some having travelled great distances, had to be turned away. To show the morbid interest in the case the *Liverpool Post* reported that, even if the court had seating for 10,000 spectators, it would have been filled.

Inside both prisoners adopted different poses as they listened to the evidence on the first charge, that of murdering Thomas Higgins. Catherine Flannagan fidgeted restlessly in her chair, frequently dabbing her eyes with a handkerchief. Margaret Higgins, however, sat motionless, leaning back with a weary look on her face, as if wishing it was all over.

92. Margaret Higgins murdered her husband Tom for the insurance money.

There could be only one verdict and when it was returned Margaret Higgins collapsed. The impression given by most reporters at the time was that the elder sister, Flannagan, carried out the offences with Higgins as a willing accomplice. Despite this, there was no doubt in anybody's minds as to the women's culpability. As the judge pointed out:

*The evidence was such as to leave no doubt on the minds of all who heard it, that you were guilty of the crime. Considering your relationship to the murdered man, to say nothing of others in whose death it is suggested you have been implicated – the murder is a crime so horrible, carried out so cruelly, so relentlessly, from motives so sordid, that it makes me shudder to think to what depths humanity is capable of sinking.*

Both were sentenced to hang *once three Sundays have passed.*

On the day sentence was pronounced a crowd of around three thousand irate individuals hissed and jeered as the van took the women away. It was later observed that had the mob had got hold of them they would most certainly have been lynched. That job, though, was reserved for the hangman.

The state executioner, Bartholomew Binns, had the reputation of botching his job through being drunk but on this occasion Binns bypassed the bar and the execution went smoothly.

Both women confessed in prison and were read tracts from the Bible by wardresses; they 'lived on' in grim wax effigies for almost a hundred years in Madame Tussaud's chamber of horrors.

**Sarah Mallinson** (No.17) was an abortionist approached by 28-year-old Louisa Brierle, who was desperately seeking a termination. Sarah's first demand for a fee of £5 was beaten down to £3. The 'operation' took place in Lower Broughton street, Salford. Louisa died from peritonitis one week later. The 50-year-old appeared completely unmoved when sentenced to death.

Those unfortunate children born out of wedlock appeared to be at great risk. **Elizabeth Lane** (No.18) from Ancoats told everyone she was going to take her illegitimate child to its father in Warrington. It was found abandoned in mud by the edge of a canal.

21-year-old **Margaret Higgins** (No.19) from Chorlton-on-Medlock murdered her illegitimate 14-month-old daughter Josephine when she took up with a new lover. The body was found in the river Medlock some 200 yards from the bridge in Cambridge Street. Margaret had a row with a new boyfriend to whom she threatened to drown herself in hopes that he would follow her and show some interest. When eventually she gave herself up to police, she told them that she had thrown the child over the wall into the river. The defence argued unsuccessfully that she'd accidentally dropped the child when climbing a wall near the river.

One strange feature of the case is that when passing sentence, the judge did not don the black cap.

*93. The respectable Mary Ann Britland who poisoned three people with mouse powder.*

Both **Mary Ann Britland** (No.20) and her neighbour, Thomas Dixon were dissatisfied with their respective spouses. Mary Ann, a neat, tidy woman and efficient housekeeper, objected to her husband, a carter and part-time barman overimbibing the amber nectar.

Thomas, a teetotaller, despised his wife's poor housekeeping, her relations and slovenly habits. He would tell anyone who would listen that she could hardly sew a button on. If cleanliness was next to godliness Mrs Dixon was a confirmed atheist.

The disillusioned couple seemed a perfect match, but with divorce difficult, the prospect of them coming together was remote. The couple's path to true love could only be reached upon the disappearance of their unwanted spouses.

Mary Ann worked at Fisher's Mill with her eldest daughter, 19-year-old Elizabeth, who still lived at home. The younger daughter, 18-year-old Suzzanah, was in service in Oldham. Thomas Dixon lived with his wife and some of her relations whom he despised.

At Christmas time in 1885, Mary Ann Britland purchased three packets of Harrison's vermin killer, a lethal concoction of strychnine and arsenic mixed with rice. She told the chemist that her home at 92, Turner Lane, Ashton-under-Lyne, was overrun with mice. It later transpired that there was only one real pest in the household, and she was out of control. Three months later Elizabeth Britland, the 19-year-old daughter, began vomiting violently and thrashing about on her bed complaining of excruciatingly severe stomach pains. Despite the attendance of a doctor she died within twenty-four hours. Her father, 44-year-old Thomas Dixon, suffered a similar fate one month later. A total of nearly £30 club money was pocketed by Mary Ann who was now free of all ties.

*95. Thomas Britland, her husband, became victim No. 2. Mary Ann disapproved of his drinking and slovenly ways.*

Once Mrs Britland was living alone, the rather naive Mrs Dixon invited the widow to spend as much time as she liked with both herself and her husband. The following month after consuming a last supper of tea, bread and butter, pickles, cauliflower, cucumber and onions, Mrs Dixon was, not surprisingly, taken ill with stomach pains. She died at 5.50 the

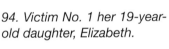

*94. Victim No. 1 her 19-year-old daughter, Elizabeth.*

following morning. Thomas Dixon picked up the best part of £20 insurance money.

A widowed neighbour was called in, for the third time in three months, to effect the unenviable task of preparing the body for burial. Mrs Dixon was therefore washed in death as she rarely was in life.

Sarah Lord had washed many corpses but none had been as stiff so soon after death as the three she attended to for Mrs Britland. She could hardly keep the matter to herself.

Gossip being as it is, the news of the stiff stiffs quickly got about, as did conjecture over the surprisingly friendly relationship between Mary Ann Britland and Thomas Dixon. Eventually the speculation resulted in an anonymous letter being sent to the police.

Three deaths in Turner Street in three months merited a visit. The police enquiries so upset Mary Ann that she virtually confessed to the funeral caterer, who called soon after the police left.

Arriving to take details as to the refreshments needed at Mrs Dixon's funeral, John Law was frantically quizzed by the disturbed Mary Ann Britland. She asked the pieman whether police could tell if somebody had been poisoned and, if they could, whether they were able to trace it to the tea she had served? The hapless caterer seemed to be well acquainted with cases of poisoning and answered in the affirmative to both questions.

Following a post-mortem that revealed Mrs Dixon had died from strychnine poisoning, Mary Ann Britland was arrested. The bodies of her husband and daughter were exhumed and death attributed to the same poison.

*96. Victim No. 3 was Mrs Dixon, the wife of her lover.*

Thomas Dixon was also arrested but subsequently discharged for lack of evidence. Mary Ann, who had bought the mouse powder, was left to face the charge of murdering Mrs Dixon alone. The cases of the other two murders were referred to during the trial, but the defendant was not charged with them.

With the evidence against her so overwhelming all in court expected a swift conviction, but after four hours the jury could not agree on a unanimous verdict. The stumbling block was that some thought Thomas Dixon was equally guilty and they did not wish to condemn Mary Ann without him.

Now well after 10pm, the judge threatened them with a night in a hotel if no decision could be reached. This quickly focused their minds and fifteen minutes later the inevitable verdict was returned.

A junior counsel takes up the story from the late night sitting:

*And now the jury return and answer to their names. The gaslights flare up. Doors swing backwards and forwards as counsel and officials come hurrying into court. From behind the javelin men crowds press eagerly forward at the back of the court, and tired faces peer through the darkness of the gallery, whence you hear murmurs and sighs of relief that at last the moment waited for is at hand.*

*The wretched woman, tottering to the front of the dock, is the colour of the parchment upon which her crime is indicted. She is asked why sentence should not be pronounced. She clings to the rails and begins slowly and firmly ' I am quite innocent. I am not guilty at all,' and then breaks into piteous sobs and tears, and the female warder holds her in position as if she were being photographed. The judge's clerk, who is stifling a yawn, has placed the black cap on his master's wig. The judge in his nasal, solemn tones gets to the sentence in as few personal words as may be. The woman shrieks out 'I never administered anything at all to Mary Dixon! Nothing whatever!'... The final prayer that the Lord may have mercy on her soul is lost in the wild, terror-stricken cries of the woman for mercy as they unfasten her fingers from the rails and carry her down the stairs towards the gaol, and her shrieks and sobs come echoing out of the stone passages below into the darkening court from which her fellow-creatures are slinking away in horror.*

Mary Ann Britland was the first woman to be hanged at Strangeways.

97. *The charismatic and probably schizophrenic Elizabeth Berry made a favourable impression on the male journalists who reported her case.*

## HELL'S ANGEL

With very few photos appearing in newspapers, the physical appearance, dress and demeanour of female defendants were put under the spotlight by reporters determined not to omit even the minutest of details.

In the days before fashion dictators decreed that women should resemble stick insects, **Elizabeth Berry** (No.21) standing two inches short of five feet, and weighing in at 9st 9lbs, had no shortage of male admirers. In February, 1887, she was on trial for her life on a charge of murder.

It appears that on this occasion the attention of the *Porcupine* reporter was firmly focused on the accused rather than the accusation:

*From the first she was accommodated with a seat and from the beginning to the very end she maintained precisely the same attitude. A rather undersized, slender woman, with a thin face and swarthy complexion, she sat placidly in the dock from morning till night, with her hands crossed one over the other, on her knees. Her general appearance was decidedly lady-like and neat.*

98. Oldham Workhouse. Elizabeth could not make ends meet on an annual salary of just £24.00.

She wore a fashionable hat and a handsome black satin dolman with embroidery… It was noted that the uncovered hand which rested all day on the other was particularly white. Her calm, unmoved composure in the dock was absolutely surprising. One was almost induced to believe that she was witnessing a trial rather than personally concerned in it herself.

On several occasions when some slightly amusing circumstance transpired she indulged in a quiet smile. Although her demeanour in the dock was not exactly one of indifference, it was certainly confident and hopeful. The interest in the trial began to intensify yesterday afternoon when all the witnesses had been disposed of and the ground was cleared for the speeches of the two learned counsel and the judge's summing-up. It was pretty soon evident that the prisoner could hope for little help from the judge, and during his cold analysis of the evidence, occasionally relieved by a touch of profound pathos, the prisoner several times wiped her lips, and it was evident to a close observer by the twitching of the mouth that a violent struggle was proceeding beneath the calm demeanour.

The pent up excitement in court was immediately relieved when the jury retired, by a general hum of suppressed conversation, which was eagerly joined in by numerous ladies present. The jury had been absent only a few minutes when silence was called, and then the foreman and the remaining jurors entered, the prisoner being led back into the dock at the same moment.

At this instant the weird silence in the court was painfully oppressive. In this terrible lull the clerk of the court in an off-handed manner contrasting singularly with the surroundings, asked the momentous question upon which hung the prisoner's existence. The faces of the jury, however, sufficiently indicated the dread message which the foreman had to deliver. The prisoner at the moment of supreme tension cast a furtive and fearful glance at the foreman, and on his uttering the word, "Guilty," she for the first time during the trial gave evidence of emotion by an involuntary movement of the head and arm. She immediately recovered her usual composure, and when asked if she had anything to say, stood up boldly and uttered a few words in a low tone, and then resumed her seat.

*Then the Judge assuming the black cap proceeded in solemn and measured terms to pass the capital sentence. The court at this time was worked up to the very highest possible pitch of restrained nervous excitement. Every eye was bent upon the solitary miserable woman at the bar, who, amid all the terrors of the situation, was still apparently composed.*

*In a few brief moments the scene was changed. Between a huge male and female warder, who indicated by a touch that she must go, the prisoner steadily left the dock, and in a few short strides from the bar to the steps she caught a last glimpse of the world. One could not help feeling how different things might have been. Instead of a desolate figure, alone and unfriended, led out of the heated atmosphere of a court of justice, to be taken to the place of execution and strangled out of existence as a punishment for a hideous and inhuman crime, she might have lived for many a year to breathe the balmy air of summer, to watch the shooting crops and waving blades of golden corn, to rejoice in the pleasures of her own innocence and virtue, and in that most God-like of all feelings, a mother's love.*

The words Elizabeth Berry uttered in a low tone were: *I may be found guilty, but the whole world cannot make me guilty.*

The convicted murderess had just three Sundays to reflect upon her thirty-one years on earth.

Most Victorians had an acquaintance with premature death and whilst still an infant, Elizabeth had lost her twin sister and father in the same year.

With money being short, as soon as she was able Elizabeth followed in her mother's footsteps and went into the mill. Even as a young girl, however, she had aspirations and desired a better life than the wages that mill work could provide.

Having trained as a nurse, she soon began mixing in slightly wealthier social circles. Elizabeth married a railwayman, Thomas Berry. Three years later, with a son and daughter, the Berry's were happily domiciled in Miles Platting.

The shadow of the grim reaper would sporadically visit Victorian households and when he called on the Berrys in July, 1881, it was Thomas's health that had failed. Elizabeth collected some £70 from an insurance policy. A mere fourteen months later another £5 was paid out following the death of her son.

Now the sole breadwinner, Elizabeth left her daughter in the care of an aunt and took up the post as head nurse at Oldham Workhouse at an annual salary of £25. Elizabeth rarely saw her daughter, Edith Annie, but regularly complained

99. Elizabeth would alternately show great kindness and cruelty to her patients.

100. *A rather stern and serious group of nurses at the workhouse hospital.*

that her daughter's clothing bills used up almost half her income.

Having twice been the beneficiary of generous insurance payments, Elizabeth took out a policy that would compensate her with £10 if her daughter died. She believed that she had also negotiated a second policy which would have paid £100 to either herself or Edith Annie, whoever lived the longest.

Like their counterparts today, Victorian insurance companies were very quick to accept cash but extremely reluctant to part with it. When eventually this second policy ought to have been actuated, it was discovered that it had not properly been completed – the devil had been in the detail.

In January 1887, as a rare treat, Elizabeth allowed her 11-year-old daughter to join her for a short break at Oldham Workhouse. A few days later Edith fell ill and was treated by a Dr Patterson and nursed by her own mother. Ever at the bedside, the attentive Elizabeth Berry would give her sick daughter a segment of orange coated in sugar to help the 'medicine' go down. It was a moot point, though as to what exactly the medicine was – were the ingredients prescribed by the doctor or Elizabeth?

One Sunday evening Dr Patterson called to find his patient writhing in agony, her eyes sunk deep into their sockets, her lips blistered, red and swollen. She was a sorry sight. Edith Annie died at five o'clock the following morning. Suspecting foul play, Dr Patterson immediately summoned a colleague from the Oldham Infirmary. At the post – mortem three doctors agreed that the 11-year-old Edith Annie Berry had died as the result of some corrosive poison, the evidence of which had been carried off in her vomit.

Elizabeth Berry was charged with having murdered her own daughter by making her swallow sulphuric acid. The newspapers now started delving into the accused's past which certainly did not help her case. They uncovered the story that Elizabeth had received £150 in a *breach of promise to marry* case brought against a curate.

She was also accused of being a flirt and reading sensational novels. More seriously, rumours had been circulating that she had killed her own mother and even her husband who, having been an invalid for two years had suddenly died. Even her son's death, which Elizabeth had attributed to his sleeping in a damp bed in Blackpool, was considered suspicious.

Indeed, such was the suspicion surrounding Mrs Berry that her mother's body, inexplicably wrapped in newspaper, was exhumed during her trial. The dead woman's stomach was found to contain poison.

The local paper, the *Oldham Chronicle*, filled page after page with details of Mrs Berry's life and personal attributes. They questioned fellow workers and discovered that she would often slap patients around the face, throw glasses at fellow nurses and lock herself in the surgery. Rumoured to be an opium taker she was, at other times, most reasonable, calm and composed.

She certainly knew how to elicit sympathy from male reporters and did so throughout her four day trial – exceptionally long for the time. Indeed, so intrigued was the *Oldham Chronicle* reporter that he wrote reams about her. In fact, had he been paid the 1d a line larger journals paid their court reporters, he could almost have retired on his earnings. And he was not alone in his enthusiasm – the only photographs the newspaper published all year were those of Mrs Berry and her daughter.

The evidence was in no way conclusive but Mrs Berry, who maintained her innocence to the end, did state in a petition that, if she was guilty, she was insane at the time.

Following her conviction a coroner's court returned a verdict of wilful murder against Elizabeth for the death of her mother. There was no chance of a reprieve, however, so the second case was not brought.

102. Edith Berry was murdered by her own mother in a most horrific and cruel manner.

101. An earlier photo of Mrs Berry and daughter. The Oldham Chronicle published just three photos throughout 1887, all relating to the murder on their doorstep.

Just one week before her execution, Mrs Berry became embroiled in an argument with her defence counsel. The bizarre dispute had nothing to do with Mr Joseph Whittaker performance in court – Elizabeth objected to his fees! The lawyer argued that he had not been paid in full and put forward a claim on Mrs Berry's possessions, then stored in Oldham Workhouse. Mrs Berry was so incensed that she wrote to the guardians:

*Dear Sirs,*
*You will know that my clothing, together with other articles are still at the workhouse. These things Mr Whittaker wishes me to give to him on the pleas that he has not been sufficiently paid for my defence. Mr Whittaker has received from me £64. In addition to this sum he has my watch and chain which are valued at £14. I have left every other article that belongs to me to Mr George Robinson to dispose of according to my instructions. He has promised to erect a stone over the grave of my darling [Edith Annie], and for this I feel exceedingly grateful. I appeal to you that none be allowed to remove a single article from the workhouse, except Mr Robinson. And a word with regard to myself. I am very sad, but at peace and in full submission to God. I think I must have loved my dear ones amiss*

*since God, either in His mercy or His jealousy, has removed them. E. Berry.*

Mrs Berry's clothes were eventually auctioned off and an extremely expensive ruby red silk ball-gown sold to a waxwork exhibition in Lime Street.

For her execution, the first at Walton Prison, Elizabeth Berry wore a black silk dress. On Monday March 14th, 1887, sand had been sprinkled over the snow so that Elizabeth would not fall prematurely. The *Oldham Chronicle* reporter takes up the story:

*Upon turning the angle of the building the wretched woman saw the gallows and upon that sight she fainted. Up to that time she had been walking slowly, repeating in a faint voice the responses as the chaplain read the prayers, but as soon as the two warders found that consciousness was leaving her they hurried their pace, and at the edge of the scaffold gave her into the hands of two male warders, by whom she was placed and supported on the drop. She recovered consciousness upon this and continued to repeat the short responses "May the Lord have mercy upon me," "Lord receive my spirit." These she uttered as they were pronounced by the chaplain who stood before her, while the executioner pinioned her feet, and adjusted the fatal noose round her neck. After the cap was drawn over her face she exclaimed in a low tone "May God forgive Dr Patterson!" These were her last words for with their utterance the bolt was drawn, and in a moment she sank below the surface of the earth out of the sight of the spectators.*

As hundreds braved the bitter cold outside, Mrs Berry was dispatched to the hereafter by the hangman, Mr Berry – no relation. It was all too much for the chaplain who, visibly distraught, fled from the scene.

Even after her death male reporters were in awe of the attractive, composed murderess who had taken the life of her daughter for financial gain. The *Chronicle's* description of the corpse was far more detailed and respectful than might have been expected:

*...The body had evidently been recently washed, as the woman's hair was damp. It had been brushed back, but not combed, and lay in a tangled disorderly mass... For all that, the expression was placid, nor was there anything indicative in its appearance that it had died in pain. An observer, who did not know the woman's history, nor how she died, would not have suspected that her end was violent, unless he had lifted the coverlet, and looked at the mark on the neck. The face, however, seemed to have grown smaller about the lower part, and the cheeks were not so full, and the same remark will apply to the lips which were closed.*

There was no peace for the wicked. Anyone and everyone had their say about the case and a phrenologist left few readers as to the doubt of her guilt. His final notes on the case read:

*Mrs Berry's ears are extremely low set, which all murderers of her class possess – a very bad sign*

103. Florence Maybrick protested her innocence to her dying day.

## 'NAUGHTY MRS MAYBRICK'

In Aigburth you must know, a little
time ago
There lived Mr Maybrick
and his wife
They were very well to do and I think
'twixt me and you
That he thought as much of her as of
his life
But December and May can ne'er
agree they say
And to that fact hangs my little tale
For Maybrick has been poisoned and
the charming Mrs M_____
Is a well attended guest in Walton gaol.

Both James and **Florence Maybrick** (No.22) were arsenic users. Florence to whiten her complexion; James as a pick-me-up, both for himself and his penis – arsenic was a form of Victorian viagra. Throughout his forties, James took up the habit of stopping off at the druggists five times a day for a quick hit in the form of an arsenic laced tonic. By the Spring of 1889, James would swallow somewhere in the region of one third of a gram per day, a very high dosage when two grams were considered lethal.

It could hardly have come as a surprise that during his post-mortem small traces of the poison were found in his liver, kidneys and intestines. There was no conclusive evidence that James had been deliberately poisoned, but the immediate finger of suspicion was pointed at his wife for several reasons, few of them scientific.

The trial of Florence Maybrick was arguably the most discussed and reported in nineteenth century England. The main reason for this was the appearance, character and behaviour of the woman in the dock.

Florence was an attractive American who sported soft curls and had a well developed bust and hips, and slender waist. 5' 3" and 27-years-old, the educated and elegant Southern Belle did not fit the preconceptions of a killer. With her good looks and rosy cheeks (she must have given up the arsenic for the trial) she resembled far more the adulteress than the murderess. She was certainly guilty of the first accusation.

The trial, overseen by a mad puritanical judge, was a clash of new world and old, the liberal 'go with the flow attitude' and the conservative stiff upper lip. Florence Maybrick stood trial as much for her openly adulterous behaviour as she did for the offence with which she was charged – the deliberate poisoning of her husband.

Born Florence Chandler, the accused met her husband on a ship sailing from New York to London. Both gave the impression they had far more money than was actually the case. Married in May 1881, they moved to Liverpool one year later. James was 42, Florence 19. A son was born in 1882 and daughter four years later. Despite money being tight, the family spent well beyond their means and by 1887 were almost broke. Florence was given an allowance of just £7 per week for food, household needs and servant's wages. This was not the sort of life she had envisaged when consenting to move to England and she secretly negotiated her own loan of some £600. She came to resent her husband's miserly ways and must

104. James Maybrick. Is this the face of the most notorious murderer in British criminal history?

have told him so as she was occasionally seen sporting the odd black eye.

Florence heard that her husband had been seeing a mistress for some twenty years. Gossip also had it that he paid £100 a year towards the upkeep of the woman and her five children. The couple henceforth slept in separate bedrooms.

Being at the height of her beauty, Florence had no shortage of male admirers and began stepping out with one Alfred Brierly, a lover nearer her own age. English women of the time would have taken every precaution to keep the affair secret. This was not in an American's nature, however, and one year, at the Grand National, she openly flaunted the new man in her life.

A fair degree of cheating was common to many Victorian marriages, but it was usually husbands playing away, mostly behind closed doors. That a wife and mother could be so open and unabashed shocked conservative society. It would be one more thing held against her at her trial.

As relations between the Maybricks deteriorated, James fell ill with pains in his head and stomach.

Aged 50, following an intestinal illness which lasted some two weeks, he died in May, 1889. He was 'nursed' throughout his illness by Florence Maybrick, though it is still debatable whether even Florence Nightingale could have saved him.

The trial focused almost as much on Florence's behaviour as it did on scientific evidence. Florence admitted that she had bought and soaked flypapers to obtain arsenic as a face wash. She had done it openly, in front of the servants, a number of whom came and volunteered evidence against her.

Possibly because of her American background, Mrs Maybrick was not popular with the domestics. The children's nurse, an appropriately named Alice Yapp, would steam open her mistresses' letters to her lover. Accordingly when Mr Maybrick died Miss Yapp was immediately suspicious.

In court the adulterous relationship was not denied and it was this that outraged the judge. In a very biased summing up, Mister Justice Fitzjames Stephen accused Florence of getting up to *degraded vices*. Nevertheless, it was to the general surprise of the press and most of those in court that, just twenty-five minutes after the last evidence was heard, the all-male jury found Florence Maybrick guilty and the judge sentenced her to hang. Three women fainted.

Half a million people, including ninety members of parliament, signed a petition to say that she should not hang. Let's join the accused in her cell awaiting the drop:

*The date of my execution was not told me in Walton jail, but I heard afterward that it was to have taken place on August 26th. On the twenty-second, while I was taking my daily exercise in the yard attached to the condemned cell, the governor, Captain Anderson, accompanied by the chief matron entered. He called me to him and with a voice which – all honour to him – trembled with emotion, said:*

*Maybrick, no commutation of sentence has come down to-day, and I consider it my duty to tell you to prepare for death.*

*Thank you governor, I replied, my conscience is clear. God's will be done.*

*The following day the Governor returned with both the chaplain and warder. He came straight to the point:*

*It is well, it is good news.*

It wasn't good news for Queen Victoria, who followed the case closely and was disappointed

105. The Maybricks home in Aigburth, Liverpool.

that Florence was not to be hanged. But prison was hardly a soft option, being particularly harsh for a woman who had previously led a comparatively luxurious lifestyle.

*I was told to take off my clothes as those I had travelled in had to be sent back to the prison in Liverpool, where they belonged.*

*When I was dressed in the uniform to which the greatest stigma and disgrace is attached, I was told to sit down. The warder then stepped quickly forward and with a pair of scissors cut off my hair to the nape of my neck... I was then weighed and my height taken. My weight was one hundred and twelve pounds, and my height five feet three inches.*

At Madame Tussauds Florence's effigy got its own room, while ironically the real thing was spending her first nine months in solitary:

*I followed the warder to a door, perhaps not more than two feet in width. She unlocked it and said 'pass in'. I stepped forward but started back in horror. Through the open door I saw, by the dim light of a small window that was never cleaned a cell seven feet by four.*

*Oh, don't put me in there, I cried, I can not bear it.*

*For answer the warder took me roughly by the shoulder, gave me a push, and shut the door. There was nothing to sit upon but the cold slate floor. I sank to my knees, I felt suffocated... My cell contained only a hammock, rolled up in the corner, and three shelves let into the wall – no table nor stall. For a seat I was compelled to place my bedclothes on the floor.*

Mrs Maybrick was forced to rise at six and breakfast on a six ounce loaf of brown whole-meal bread and three-quarters of a pint of gruel. Her day was spent scrubbing the cell, sewing (one shirt per day) and knitting. The routine was only broken by a religious service and one hour's daily exercise.

Florence was released after fifteen years and returned to the States, where she went on the lecture circuit appealing for prison reform. Interest in her case soon waned. Never re-united with her children, she became an eccentric recluse befriending stray dogs and cats. She died of a stroke in obscurity and poverty in a shack in rural Connecticut in 1941. This, however, was not the end of the story.

Just over half a century after her death, Florence Maybrick was hitting the headlines again. In 1992, a book, professing to be the diary of Jack the Ripper, was published. It was received with a certain amount of skepticism from Ripperologists and historians alike but, over the years, it has gained credibility among those fascinated by the Whitechapel murders. What connection has the diary, you may be wondering, with the Liverpool Poisoning case? It was signed by none other than James Maybrick.

According to the diary, Maybrick took his revenge for his wife's flaunted adultery by slashing the throats of five prostitutes in London's East End. Maybrick rented a flat on Petticoat Lane and would often spend weekends (all the murders were committed on Friday, Saturday or Sunday) in the capital. Many reasons are given as to why Maybrick could have been the serial killer and as many as to why he was not.

Maybrick may in fact have been Jack the Ripper, in which case Florence, if she was guilty of murder, indirectly saved the lives of many working girls. There are just far too many 'ifs' and 'buts' and the likelihood that two of the most notorious murder cases of Victorian times are interwoven is just a little too neat. For two infamous murderers to be

106. Mrs Maybrick after her release. She died a recluse in Connecticut in 1941.

living under the same roof stretches credulity to breaking point. Even so...

Unlike the above crime, those that follow merited mere notes in the court reports.

25-year-old **Jane Jones** (No.23) was another servant who could not afford babyminding fees and drowned her six-month-old son in the sea off Fleetwood. She was again pregnant at her trial. **Elizabeth Mapp** (No.24) gave birth in Stockport workhouse and threw her baby into the Mersey.

## ALL SOLICITORS ARE ROGUES

A failed breach of promise case in 1894 led a very determined, and probably very sick woman, to take the law into her own hands, with fatal consequences.

Some two years after judgment against her, 32-year-old **Catherine Kempshall** (No.25) glared across the plush boardroom in the offices in Water Street, Liverpool. She had been pursuing Edgar Holland with dogged determination and this was to be the final showdown. Holland was desperate to rid himself of the woman and proposed that, although she had no legal or moral claim, he would make a financial settlement and told her to see her solicitors. The mere mention of anybody in that profession was like red rag to a bull for Catherine. She screamed back at him across the polished table:

*I want no solicitors. All solicitors are rogues. I want you to pay me. You promised to marry me and to leave me at your property to compensate me for my losses and for all the wrongs you have done me.*

The exasperated businessman insisted:

*I never promised to marry you. I never wronged you. I have always treated you with kindness.*

This was too much for Catherine who, screaming the words *you haven't you beast* drew out a revolver from under her cloak and discharged four bullets at the the man she had once loved.

The mortally wounded man's own solicitor, Alsop, was also in the room and rushed to disarm the demented gunwoman. At this point, like something from a penny dreadful, Catherine unsheathed a knife and lunged at a member of the profession she so despised. The fight was halted by the timely appearance of the dying Edgar Holland's brother. Catherine was disarmed and ordered to sit in a chair while the police were summoned.

With three bullets in his chest the wounded Holland wanted shot of the demented Kempshall:

*Will you take this woman out of my sight as soon as possible. I cannot bear the sight of her.*

Catherine was going nowhere and calmly sat watching the man writhing in agony. She told the policeman: *Oh I wont run away.*

Edgar Holland died from his wounds two months later.

The following spring large numbers of spectators were turned away from Catherine's murder trial as all vacant seats were swiftly snapped up.

At a time when the accused could neither be cross-examined nor give evidence in their own defence, Catherine pleaded 'not guilty' in a loud voice, dismissed the protestations of her counsel with a curt *shut up* and pleaded her case:

*It is my only chance to speak. I did not kill him. He rushed at me to take the revolver away and it went off in the struggle. Alsop [the solicitor witness] is a liar and it would not be his profession if he wasn't.*

Asked if she objected to any of the jurymen being sworn in she rather logically replied: *I don't know them. I hope they are none of Holland's men.*

After the said jury had heard a witness testify that Catherine had promised to shoot Holland like a dog if he would not agree her terms, they quickly found her guilty but with a recommendation to mercy. Catherine, when asked if she had anything to say in mitigation, told the court that she had the gun to shoot herself but the judge was having none of this fiction and sentenced her to hang.

To most of those present it was obvious that Catherine Kempshall was not completely of sound mind and nearly 18,000 signed a petition that she should not hang. The signatories even included members of the family of the man she had shot. One man who did not sign saying *You fools, I'd hang her twice* was chased down Dale Street by an umbrella-and basket-wielding band of female petitioners.

Meanwhile, in prison, Catherine implored her solicitor to smuggle in some poison so, she said, she could bleach her hair and surprise the prison authorities. Catherine's mental health was clearly deteriorating and, whilst awaiting death, she spent the nights laughing hysterically, screaming wildly and singing broken snatches of songs in a tuneless manner. During the day she capered about the cell in a demented fashion. When told that she had been reprieved and was to be sent to Broadmoor she received the news with complete indifference.

A few days prior to her departure she was given some 'good' books by a wardress as she had not attended the prison chapel. Catherine took one look at the titles which included *The Devout Christian* and flew off into another one of her rages.

*The people who write these books are a set of canting humbugs and don't know what they are writing about. If they had been in the hell that I have been in for the last five years they would not have written such rubbish.*

Maybe Catherine was not so mad after all.

**Isabella Cookson** (No.26) threw her unwanted granddaughter over a fence onto a tip in Preston. The newly born infant died of exposure.

# MURDER GUIDE TO LANCASHIRE

**1 BARROW** Mary Ann Doyle drowned her 4-year-old son and attempted suicide as she could not get along with her mother-in-law.

**2 LANCASTER** In 1872 Mary Davidson got off the train to Carlisle and drowned her daughter. She feared her new sweetheart would dump her if he discovered she had a child.

**3 FLEETWOOD** Jane Jones, a domestic servant, threw her baby into the sea. She was again pregnant at her trial.

**4 SOUTHPORT** Elizabeth Scott posted her ten-day-old son to Stalybridge.

**5 PRESTON** In 1858 Jane Parker sent her new-born baby in a box to Liverpool. The baby was still clinging on to life when the box was opened but died at the hospital. Isabella Cookson threw her granddaughter onto a tip.

**6 COLNE** Harriett Rushton, a sober and respectable woman, strangled her three young children and spent the rest of her life in an asylum.

**7 OLDHAM** Elizabeth Berry poisoned her 11-year-old daughter and probably other members of her family. Hanged by the executioner, Mr Berry, in 1887.

**8 ASHTON-UNDER-LYNE** Mary Ann Britland used mouse powder as a form of pest control. The pests were two members of her own family and her lover's wife. The first woman to be hanged at Strangeways.

**9 STOCKPORT** Mary Bennett seemed to think she had done nothing wrong. She told the court: 'I did not do anything with the child except put it in the water.' Elizabeth Mapp threw her baby into the Mersey.

**10 SALFORD** Home to the abortionist Sarah Mollinson who appeared completely unmoved when sentenced to death following a botched 'operation'.

**11 MANCHESTER** Several child murders. Elizabeth Lane abandoned her baby by a canal in Ancoats. Margaret Higgins threw her baby into the Medlock.

**12 WIDNES** Mary Ann Tracey and two male accomplices murdered her husband. Both men hanged but Mary Ann was spared the rope as she was pregnant.

**13 BOOTLE** Mary Williams was hanged for shooting a neighbour. Two teenage domestic servants murdered a former employer and admired themselves in the mirror sporting the dead woman's clothes.

**14 LIVERPOOL** The Borgias sisters murdered members of their family for the insurance money. Florence Maybrick was found guilty of murdering her husband who some believe may have been Jack the Ripper. Sophia Todd advertised her services as a baby farmer and swiftly disposed of her charges. Ellen Lanigan abandoned her new-born twins. Catherine Kempshall shot the man who she said had proposed marriage and then changed his mind.

| | |
|---|---|
| Ac | Accrington |
| As | Aston under Lyne |
| Bp | Bacup |
| Ec | Eccles |
| Ha | Haslingden |
| He | Heywood |
| MA | MANCHESTER |
| Mi | Middleton |
| Mo | Mossley |
| OL | OLDHAM |
| Pr | Prestwich |
| Ra | Radcliffe |
| RO | ROCHDALE |
| Rw | Rawtenstall |
| SA | SALFORD |
| St | Stretford |
| Sw | Swinton and Pendlbury |

| | |
|---|---|
| WIGAN | County boroughs |
| Eccles | Municipal Boroughs |

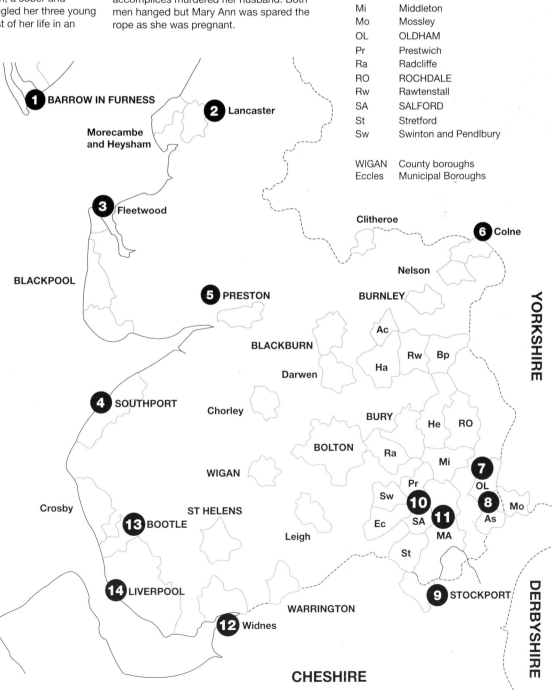

Nos 27 and 28 were young domestic servants who smothered an elderly lady with her pillows as she lay in her bed. The victim, Miss Marsden, had been chosen by 20-year-old **Ethel Rollinson** (No.27) who had been in the service of the hard-drinking 71 year-old Bootle woman for one month.

After the murder, the girls tried on the victim's hats and admired themselves in the mirror. They were caught when trying to pawn some of the stolen clothes. The jury was out just half-an-hour and both girls had to be carried from the court semi-conscious after sentence of death was passed.

One strange feature of the case was that 17-year-old **Eva Eastwood,** (No.28) whilst awaiting the outcome of a petition in Walton gaol, was re-united with her estranged mother, also serving a stretch. Eva and her family had long believed her mum to be dead. The newspaper reported *and the interview which ensued was of a most touching and effecting nature.*

**Mary Ann Boyle** (No.29) stood in the dock following a failed suicide bid. Along with her 4-year-old son, she was pulled out of three feet of water in a lock in Barrow. She survived but her son later died. Mary had been forced to live with her drunken foul-mouthed mother-in-law and lazy husband, who had worked just six weeks of the preceding two years. The son, James, had been born to a different father before the marriage. Prior to her suicide attempt Mary Ann wrote to her mother:

*You will be surprised when you get this as I know you have much trouble, but I am writing this on my way to the grave. No-one to blame, only Mrs Boyle – from your daughter – so goodbye as I intend to end my sorrow. Come over and get my things.*

**Mary Ellen Moore** (No.30) was a waitress who insisted her baby daughter had been born ill and died of natural causes. This was proved to be a lie when paper was found in the poor child's throat.

---

## ACKNOWLEDGEMENTS

Librarians vary from the super efficient and helpful in places like Oldham, to the indifferent jobsworths in other towns which shall remain anonymous. Thankfully most in Lancashire fell into the first category. Many thanks for your time and invaluable help.

Duncan and Dave at the Manchester Police Museum found time to provide photos and advice. The Museum has improved enormously over the last few years and is well worth a visit.

Viv Foster again tidied up the text and told me off though we didn't have our usual heated arguments, we must be getting old.

Anybody wishing to do further research over this period might be interested in the collections of oral history tapes at Lancaster University and Clitheroe.

## ILLUSTRATION ACKNOWLEDGEMENTS

**GREATER MANCHESTER POLICE MUSEUM:**
*29, 30, 48, 49, 50, 51, 54, 57, 58, 59, 60, 62, 63, 64, 65, 66, 67, 69, 76, 77, 83, 84.*

**THE ILLUSTRATED POLICE NEWS:**
*1, 17, 18, 61, 74, 85, 86, 87, 88, 89, 90.*

**THE OLDHAM CHRONICLE:**
*97, 101, 102.*

**WIGAN HERITAGE SERVICE**
*27, 28, 33, 34, 35, 36, 37, 38, 40, 42, 43.*

**THE SALVATION ARMY:**
*16, 31, 53, 56, 72, 75.*

**THE LOCAL STUDIES/LEISURE SERVICES:**
**LIVERPOOL:**
*3, 6, 8, 9, 10, 11, 12, 13, 14, 19, 21, 52, 55, 71.*

**SALFORD:**
*2, 15, 24, 26, 70, 73.*

**LANCASTER:**
*7, 23, 45, 47.*

**OLDHAM:**
*20, 39, 44, 68, 98, 99, 100.*

**ACCRINGTON:**
*22, 41.*

**CHORLEY:**
*25, 32, 46.*

**SEFTON:**
*78, 79, 80, 81, 82.*

*All other photos from the author's collection.*

# CRIMINAL AND SOCIAL HISTORY THEY DIDN'T DARE TEACH YOU AT SCHOOL!

**TITLE: LONDON... THE SINISTER SIDE**
AUTHOR: **STEVE JONES**
ISBN: **1-87000-000-5**
SIZE: **A4**
PAGES: **88**
ILLUSTRATIONS/PHOTOS: **104**
PRICE: **£6.99**
NOTES: **AVAILABLE IN JAPANESE**

Our first and best-selling book which has been in print since 1986 with reprints well into double figures. Topics covered range from early executions to the Kray Twins. 15 pages are devoted to the hunt for Jack the Ripper and the book illustrated with over 100 photographs and pictures.

**TITLE: WICKED LONDON**
AUTHOR: **STEVE JONES**
ISBN: **1-870000-01-3**
SIZE: **A4**
PAGES: **96**
ILLUSTRATIONS/PHOTOS: **96**
PRICE: **£6.99**
NOTES: **AVAILABLE IN JAPANESE.**

In two parts. The first half of the book examines the most notorious murder cases in the capital including Dr. Crippen, Christie, Haigh - 'the acid-bath' murderer and many more. The second half is centred around social life - food, drink and leisure - and conflict within the capital, including chapters on the often violent struggle of the women's movement and tragic tales of the Blitz.

**TITLE: THROUGH THE KEYHOLE**
AUTHOR: **STEVE JONES**
ISBN: **1-870000-02-1**
SIZE: **A4**
PAGES: **104**
ILLUSTRATIONS/PHOTOS: **109**
PRICE: **£6.99**
NOTES: **AVAILABLE IN JAPANESE**

A peek at private lives, from prince to pauper, in the eighteenth and nineteenth centuries. 'Through the Keyhole' reveals the secrets of what went on behind locked doors in workhouses, slums and palaces - with detailed court accounts of adultery and sexual scandal. In later chapters we look at how the masses spent their limited leisure time in pubs and penny playhouses.

**TITLE: CAPITAL PUNISHMENTS**
AUTHOR: **STEVE JONES**
ISBN: **1-870000-03-X**
SIZE: **A4**
PAGES: **104**
ILLUSTRATIONS/PHOTOS: **106**
PRICE: **£7.99**
NOTES: **AVAILABLE IN JAPANESE.**

A detailed look at a variety of cases coming before the 'beak' in Victorian times. Assault and wife-beating were only too common following serious sessions in the ale-houses. The book follows those convicted into the horrors of the Victorian prison system where silence was often the rule and the food 'scarce fit for hogs'. Many of the stories of the atrocious conditions are related by the prisoners themselves.

**TITLE: IN DARKEST LONDON**
AUTHOR: **STEVE JONES**
ISBN: **1-870000-04-8**
SIZE: **A4**
PAGES: **88**
ILLUSTRATIONS/PHOTOS: **79**
PRICE: **£6.99**

The book covers the period 1900-39 and relates first hand stories of prostitutes, criminals and backstreet abortionists. Details of the bombing raids in world war one are followed by tales of the General Strike of 1926 and an in depth look at Mosley's racist marches in the East End that resulted in serious violence and disruption. Light relief is provided with the extraordinary life of the prostitute's padre who ended his days in a lion's cage.

**TITLE: WHEN THE LIGHTS WENT DOWN**
AUTHOR: **STEVE JONES**
ISBN: **1-870000-05-6**
SIZE: **A4**
PAGES: **104**
ILLUSTRATIONS/PHOTOS: **91**
PRICE: **£7.99**

We've all heard the stories about the civilian population during WW2 pulling together, singing patriotic songs in crowded air-raid shelters and accepting the wartime privations in good heart. Indeed many did, but there was a sizeable minority who were determined to help themselves rather than their country. German bombers facilitated entry to other people's houses, and undercover of the blackout, looters set out on their gruesome treasure trove. Both crime figures and the prison population rose as offenders from black-marketeers to murderers sought to profit from the chaotic conditions.

**TITLE: NOTTINGHAM... THE SINISTER SIDE**
AUTHOR: **STEVE JONES**
ISBN: **1-870000-06-4**
SIZE: **A4**
PAGES: **104**
ILLUSTRATIONS/PHOTOS: **110**
PRICE: **£7.99**

Although internationally famous for being the home of Britain's most famous outlaw, Robin Hood, Nottingham, like all large cities, has housed tens of thousands of lawbreakers with no intention whatsoever of giving to the poor. The most infamous murderers include 'Nurse' Waddingham who poisoned two of her patients for their inheritance, and Herbert Mills, who executed 'the perfect murder' in order to sell his story to the newspapers - both were hanged.

**TITLE: MANCHESTER... THE SINISTER SIDE**
AUTHOR: **STEVE JONES**
ISBN: **1-870000-09-9**
SIZE: **A4**
PAGES: **104**
ILLUSTRATIONS/PHOTOS: **103**
PRICE: **£6.99**

NOTES: **THE FIRST OF TWO BOOKS ON THE CITY.**
**THIS ONE DEALS WITH CRIME AND SOCIAL HISTORY UP TO 1914**

In the nineteenth century Manchester's reputation for crime and depravity was second only to London. Join us in a trip through the slums, gin houses and brothels of the city to witness the atrocious living conditions that in part led to the high levels of crime. Many of the photos of criminals are from the Manchester Police Museum and published for the first time.

**TITLE: BIRMINGHAM...THE SINISTER SIDE**
AUTHOR: **STEVE JONES**
ISBN: **1-870000-14-5**
SIZE: **A4**
PAGES: **104**
ILLUSTRATIONS/PHOTOS: **133**
PRICE: **£7.99**

NOTES: **THIS BOOK IS EXTREMELY POPULAR,**
**THE FIRST PRINT SELLING OUT IN ELEVEN WEEKS.**
**HAS BEEN FEATURED ON SEVERAL RADIO AND**
**TELEVISION PROGRAMMES.**

'Pickpockets, petty thieves, prostitutes, drunks, murderers and wife-beaters galore people its pages staring back at the reader from police 'mug-shots' with grim resignation, pathos or rebellion in their eyes sandwiched between spine-chilling 'penny-dreadful' illustrations portraying scenes of red murder of callous brutality, each of which for a fleeting moment in time, shocked the un-shockable!' (Black Country Bugle)

**TITLE: NORTHUMBERLAND AND DURHAM...**
        **THE SINISTER SIDE**
AUTHOR: **STEVE JONES**
ISBN: **1-870000-49-8**
SIZE: **A4**
PAGES: **104**
ILLUSTRATIONS/PHOTOS: **100**
PRICE: **£7.99**

With tales from Berwick to Darlington, petty-theft to mass-murder join us in an uncensored trip back to Victorian times in Northumberland and old County Durham. Stories of Britain's wickedest woman plus many tales from the courtrooms, slums and ale-houses so popular in the North-East.

# WICKED PUBLICATIONS

Lavishly illustrated and studiously researched, our original stories and photographs would certainly interest students (GCSE to degree level), local historians, social historians, genealogists and criminologists - but above all they are aimed at the general reader.

To date our satisfied customers total over 250,000.

## TERMS AND CONDITIONS

### INDIVIDUAL SALES

We supply orders to the general public at the prices listed below. Wicked Publications pay all postage and packing within the U.K. and books will be sent within twenty-four hours of an order being received. Cheques should be made payable to **Wicked Publications**. At the moment we cannot accept credit cards. If you would like the books signed or dedicated please mention this with the order.

### BUSINESS

We have accounts with all major booksellers and museum/visitor shops. Our general terms are 35% sale or return, if they don't sell we will take the book back if in resalable condition. We can confidently make this promise as returns over ten years have been minimal. We may give better terms for large orders or swift payment or to regular customers, everything is negotiable, please phone.

---

# ORDER FORM

PLEASE SEND ORDER ALONG WITH CHEQUE TO **WICKED PUBLICATIONS AT 222, HIGHBURY ROAD, BULWELL, NOTTINGHAM NG6 9FE ENGLAND. TEL: 0115 975 6828**

| TITLE | PRICE | NO OF COPIES |
|---|---|---|
| LONDON... THE SINISTER SIDE | £6.99 | |
| WICKED LONDON | £6.99 | |
| THROUGH THE KEYHOLE | £6.99 | |
| CAPITAL PUNISHMENTS | £7.99 | |
| IN DARKEST LONDON | £6.99 | |
| WHEN THE LIGHTS WENT DOWN | £7.99 | |
| NOTTINGHAM... THE SINISTER SIDE | £7.99 | |
| MANCHESTER... THE SINISTER SIDE | £6.99 | |
| BIRMINGHAM... THE SINISTER SIDE | £7.99 | |
| NORTHUMBERLAND AND DURHAM... THE SINISTER SIDE | £7.99 | |
| *Postage (where applicable) | £ | *(ALL POSTAGE IS FREE WITHIN THE U.K. ADD £1.50 PER BOOK MAINLAND EUROPE AND £3 U.S.A, CANADA, AUSTRALIA AND NEW ZEALAND). |
| TOTAL | £ | |

Name ..................................................................

Address ...............................................................

..........................................................................

..........................................................................

.......................... Post Code .....................